M. Night Shyamalan: Interviews

Conversations with Filmmakers Series
Gerald Peary, General Editor

M. NIGHT SHYAMALAN

INTERVIEWS

Edited by Adrian Gmelch

University Press of Mississippi / Jackson

The University Press of Mississippi is the scholarly publishing agency of
the Mississippi Institutions of Higher Learning: Alcorn State University,
Delta State University, Jackson State University, Mississippi State University,
Mississippi University for Women, Mississippi Valley State University,
University of Mississippi, and University of Southern Mississippi.

www.upress.state.ms.us

The University Press of Mississippi is a member
of the Association of University Presses.

Copyright © 2023 by University Press of Mississippi
All rights reserved

First printing 2023
∞

Library of Congress Cataloging-in-Publication Data

Names: Gmelch, Adrian, 1993– editor.
Title: M. Night Shyamalan : interviews / Adrian Gmelch.
Other titles: Conversations with filmmakers series.
Description: Jackson : University Press of Mississippi, 2023. | Series: Conversations
    with filmmakers series | Includes bibliographical references and index.
Identifiers: LCCN 2023014351 (print) | LCCN 2023014352 (ebook) |
    ISBN 9781496848024 (hardback) | ISBN 9781496848031 (trade paperback) |
    ISBN 9781496848048 (epub) | ISBN 9781496848055 (epub) |
    ISBN 9781496848062 (pdf) | ISBN 9781496848079 (pdf)
Subjects: LCSH: Shyamalan, M. Night—Interviews. | Motion picture producers and
    directors—United States—Interviews. | Screenwriters—United States—Interviews.
Classification: LCC PN1998.3.S485 A5 2023 (print) | LCC PN1998.3.S485 (ebook) |
    DDC 791.4302/33092—dc23/eng/20230517
LC record available at https://lccn.loc.gov/2023014351
LC ebook record available at https://lccn.loc.gov/2023014352

British Library Cataloging-in-Publication Data available

Contents

Introduction   ix

Chronology   xiii

Filmography   xv

Shyamalan's Indian Summer   3
    Anne Thompson / 1993

Dawn of Night   5
    Carrie Rickey / 1998

Extrasensory Perception   12
    Stephen Pizzello / 2000

Out of This World   19
    Jeff Giles / 2002

The Director of Fear   27
    David Denby / 2002

Dark Prince   35
    Rachel Abramowitz / 2004

Blue Scare: Shyamalan's Winning Recipes   43
    Gérard Delorme / 2004

Shyamalan's Take   49
    Carrie Rickey / 2006

M. Night Shyamalan: The Art of the Creepy Movie   53
   Neal Conan / 2006

Persistence of Vision   61
   Leonard Guercio / 2008

Another Happening from Director M. Night Shyamalan   66
   Brad Balfour / 2008

The Last Airbender: Roundtable Discussion with M. Night Shyamalan   71
   Cloneweb.net / 2010

M. Night Shyamalan: Seeing Signs   87
   Knowledge at Wharton / 2011

The Shyamalans: An Exclusive Interview with the Main Line Power Couple   94
   Melissa Jacobs / 2014

How to Master the Supernatural   98
   Matt Blake / 2015

"The Only Thing That Matters to Me Is What I Think about My Own Films"   103
   Gauthier Jurgensen / 2015

M. Night Shyamalan Interview: *Split*, Nonconformity, Creative Freedom   108
   Ryan Lambie / 2017

Superheroes as a Disease of Cinema? M. Night Shyamalan Interviewed about *Glass*   115
   Matthias Hopf / 2019

M. Night Shyamalan Reflects on the Evolution of His Career, His Filmmaking Philosophy, and That *Old* Ending   121
   Steve Weintraub / 2021

Jury President M. Night Shyamalan: "The Berlinale Is a Mini Film School"   130
   Andreas Busche / 2022

"Terrorized by This Light in Us"   134
   Aurélian Lemant / 2022

Further Reading   141

Index   143

Introduction

M. Night Shyamalan's career got off to an unfortunate start with his first major studio film, *Wide Awake* (1998), an improbable religious-themed family comedy. But one year after, the box office hit *The Sixth Sense* brought Shyamalan immense success, name recognition, and instant fandom. So unusual for a supernatural thriller, this film was nominated for six Academy Awards, including Best Picture, Best Director, and Best Screenplay. Though he came close to capturing the magic with *Unbreakable* (2000) and *Signs* (2002), there was little chance the Indian American filmmaker could live up to the enormous expectations placed on him thereafter.

Instead? With *The Village* (2004), Shyamalan became a scapegoat of critics, and *Lady in the Water* (2006) was both a critical and financial failure. Curiously, though many of his films—*The Happening* (2008), *The Last Airbender* (2010), and *After Earth* (2013)—were poorly reviewed, a creative dry spell, these works usually managed to be profitable. Shyamalan's intense fan base has never abandoned him. If there has never quite been another *The Sixth Sense*, Shyamalan returned to artistic prominence with *The Visit* (2015), *Split* (2016), and *Glass* (2019), and the box office was huge for Universal Pictures. His next film, *Old* (2021), had a more mixed reception.

It is instructive and fascinating to have a close look at interviews with the filmmaker. The first aspect that shines through almost every meeting with Shyamalan is his strong and unbending self-confidence. Words that are mentioned when describing the filmmaker are "cocky" (Giles 2002), "boundless confidence" and "chutzpah" (Pizzello 2000), "jaunty assurance" (Abramowitz 2004), and "cocksureness" (Rickey 2006). This self-assurance some interpret as arrogance, but more of his interviewers are impressed by a second aspect of Shyamalan: his enthusiastic and optimistic demeanor. He is a pleasant person to talk to.

Gérard Delorme describes the filmmaker: "All of Shyamalan's philosophy is contained in this positive, voluntaristic, vaguely New-Age approach" (2004). And Shyamalan himself: "I genuinely think everybody is great. I really am a positive guy" (Wharton 2011). Although his films are often very dark, they are also about nurturing and healing self-discovery, about reaching one's full potential, about finding one's voice. Shyamalan's positive worldview might be a reason why—after severe criticism and box-office failures—he maintained faith in himself and his capabilities. He sees himself as a "believer." As Delorme explains it: "For Shyamalan, chance is good. Every event, good or bad, is a sign of destiny that one must know how to interpret."

The third striking aspect of Shyamalan is his talent for self-promotion, he acting at times like a PR professional. He has been deeply involved in the marketing of his films and has turned his name into a brand, like Alfred Hitchcock or Steven Spielberg.

The fourth aspect is his important connection to his wife, Dr. Bhavna Vaswani, who has greatly influenced him. She is mentioned in nearly every interview, and together they founded in 2001 the M. Night Shyamalan Foundation to fight world poverty. One double interview with Shyamalan and Vaswani is found in this book (Jacobs 2014), demonstrating her importance.

Vaswani is a therapist and clinical development psychologist—and Shyamalan has a strong penchant for psychology in his movies: psychologists and psychiatrists are recurring characters, sanatoriums frequent settings, illnesses and neuroses abiding motifs. And there is the psychologizing of his characters across all of his cinema. The protagonists of his films are in store for traumatic experiences, and they will be marked and scarred by these experiences.

And yet, at the end of Shyamalan's films, they mostly escape their traumas; their psychological shock has led to their healing. Shyamalan does the same as his wife, the psychologist: he gives his (fictional) patients the necessary psychological help to cure them. Think, for example, of Dr. Crowe (*The Sixth Sense*), who, though blinded by trauma, finally is able to accept his death. Think of Graham Hess (*Signs*), who finds in the end the faith lost through trauma. Think of Cleveland (*Lady in the Water*), whose mental suffering is healed.

The fifth aspect of Shyamalan is his shaky relationship with the studio system. He lives in the Philadelphia area and shoots most of his films there. It's rare in interviews that he doesn't indulge in an opportunity to address his distance and independence from the industry in Los Angeles. Carrie Rickey writes in 1998 that the filmmaker is "so resistant to going Hollywood that he is bringing Hollywood to Philadelphia." That hasn't changed through the years, as he told Andreas Busche in 2022: "I've always seen myself as an independent director working within the structures of Hollywood. I'm 3,000 miles away from the film industry here in Philadelphia, and I've been financing my films myself lately."

Shyamalan is recognized by journalists and critics for finding a viable compromise between films for the art house and those for the masses. Shyamalan: "I want it to be a phenomenon—a cultural phenomenon, where the audience feels some connection to this place, these people and what was being said here. That's *Jaws*, *E.T.*, *The Exorcist*. All those movies. They just *connected*" (Giles 2002). That's his mainstream aspiration. At the same time, Shyamalan proclaims: "My goal has always been to create something of my own, something original . . . I feel a great affinity with independent cinema and world cinema, with forms of storytelling that dare to do something new." The filmmaker always tries to captivate with thoughtful and intelligent staging: color codes, lighting effects, reflections, complex camera movements. While the story or the topics dealt with are sometimes less than subtle, the accompanying mise-en-scène is deeply complex, conveying atmosphere and emotion.

Shyamalan favors stories with ordinary middle-class people as heroes. They are thrown into bizarre, sometimes supernatural life-threatening situations that reveal their real capabilities and powers, and their ability to fight back with creative know-how. Many of his plots are family-driven, with important roles for children. The core theme of so many films is the family's cohesion, its value, its threat, its decay. There are elements of spirituality and faith mixed in with the supernatural. Whether it's horror, science fiction, superhero cinema, fantasy or disaster film, Shyamalan turns genre conventions upside down, plays with them, and combines them with serious-minded concerns such as communication (*The Sixth Sense*), love (*The Village*), storytelling (*Lady in the Water*), forgiveness (*The Visit*), or aging (*Old*).

Shyamalan's staging and cinematic style can be described as "calm" and "methodical." He has a "slow" cinematic signature, which he achieves through held shots and long pauses in conversations. The French film scholar Emmanuel Burdeau notes that Shyamalan has virtually reinvented slow storytelling in film, an insight seconded by other critics: "[H]is films . . . offer a respite from the helter-skelter speed of modern living. Shyamalan's world moves slowly, decisively" (Abramowitz 2004).

His films also show a compositional classicism and formal rigor that Shyamalan borrowed from one of his idols, Alfred Hitchcock. It makes sense for the filmmaker to be called the "Hitchcock of the supernatural thriller."[1] The majority of Shyamalan's films are confined to narrow "home" spaces (be it a house, an apartment complex, a village, a tightly confined environment). The films come alive through their spatial restriction. And last, the plot twist has become his trademark, a "shock" to the system. But sentimentality and emotion are far more important to Shyamalan than explicit violence or sex (never shown in a film to date). Unlike Hitchcock, Shyamalan is definitely not a voyeuristic filmmaker.

Finally, Shyamalan's films refer to each other, they are cross-referenced. Sometimes it's colors, sometimes it's setting, sometimes it's characters, sometimes it's story, sometimes it's a tracking shot that ties the various films together. For

---

1 David Bordwell, *The Way Hollywood Tells It: Story and Style in Modern Movies* (Los Angeles: University of California Press, 2006), 54.

those familiar with the filmmaker's complete body of work, this is a fascinating experience to feel the echoes resounding within.

Let's finish with one obsession particularly important for Shyamalan: his artistic integrity. He advises to "work on your authenticity, your own voice" (Wharton 2011), he explains to "crush (your ego) and then what's left is something pure; the pure artist" (Blake 2015). And what is the life of the artist of integrity? "My perfect day is, I read a book, I work a little bit at home, very quiet, and then I go down to my theatre and watch a great, classic movie, like a gem" (Lambie 2017).

For this book, I tried to select one interview for each important period in Shyamalan's life, from early reportages by Rickey (1998) and Giles (2002) through interviews that provide insight into Shyamalan's recent work (such as Lambie 2017 or Lemant 2022). Not limiting myself to English-language interviews, I looked to Europe for interesting conversations with Shyamalan. These texts from French and German sources are here translated into English for the first time. The interest in Shyamalan has always been great in Europe, and his films, even the so-called weaker ones, have received far more praise in France and Germany than in the United States. For example, two heavily criticized films in the US, *The Village* (2004) and *Lady in the Water* (2006), each landed on the list of the best films of the year in the renowned French film magazine *Cahiers du cinéma*, respectively ranked second and sixth. In a word, M. Night Shyamalan is, abroad, a major "auteur." May this collection of interviews bring the talented, brilliant filmmaker into the same high rank in the United States.

My thanks go to, especially, Carrie Rickey, Jeff Giles, Stephen Pizzello, Gérard Delorme, Brad Balfour, Leonard Guerico, Matt Blake, Ryan Lambie, Matthias Hopf, Steve Weintraub, Andreas Busche, and Thomas Aïdan, who allowed me to use their interviews and conversations. I also want to thank Dr. Heinz Gmelch and, at the University Press of Mississippi, Emily Bandy. This book would not have been possible without their help.

AG

Chronology

1970   Born Manoj Nelliyattu Shyamalan on August 6 in Mahé, Pondicherry, India, to Nelliate C. and Jayalakshmi Shyamalan, both doctors.
1988   New York University Merit Scholarship.
1992   Graduates from New York University Tisch School of the Arts; *Praying with Anger* released, which premieres at the Toronto International Film Festival.
1993   *Praying with Anger* wins the "First Film Competition" for American independent filmmakers at the AFI Fest; Shyamalan marries wife Bhavna.
1994   Sells his script *Labor of Love* to 20th Century Fox, but it's never made into a film.
1995   Filming *Wide Awake*, dispute with Harvey Weinstein, who delays the release and lets the film languish in "postproduction hell."
1998   *Wide Awake* finally released; Shyamalan founds own production company, Blinding Edge Pictures.
1999   *The Sixth Sense* released; nominated for Academy Awards for Best Director and Best Screenplay, nominated for Writers Guild of America Awards for best screenplay, awarded Bram Stoker Award for best screenplay and Nebula Award for best script; international breakthrough with a $672 million box office score
2000   *Unbreakable* released; positive reviews but not the hoped-for box-office success; develops a cult following over the years.
2001   Launches together with his wife, Bhavna, the M. Night Shyamalan Foundation, which has set itself the goal of fighting poverty and social injustice.
2002   *Signs* released, which becomes Shyamalan's second-most popular box office hit, with $408.2 million grossed; Shyamalan on the cover of *Newsweek*.
2004   *The Village* released; fake documentary *The Buried Secret of M. Night Shyamalan* (produced by Shyamalan himself) makes controversy.
2006   *Lady in the Water* released by Warner Bros. Pictures after Shyamalan breaks his longtime collaboration with Disney since *The Sixth Sense*;

	the film is received harshly by most critics and is a box office failure; publishes children's book *Lady in the Water*; first commercial shot for American Express; named ShoWest Director of the Year.
2008	*The Happening* released; awarded the Padma Shri from Indian government for his distinguished contribution to cinema.
2010	*The Last Airbender* released, an adaptation of the animated television series *Avatar: The Last Airbender*; the film is again heavily criticized; Shyamalan produces *Devil*, which was intended to be the first work of a horror film trilogy under the name The Night Chronicles.
2013	*After Earth* released, which is also panned by critics and stops Shyamalan's collaboration with major Hollywood studios; publishes *I Got Schooled* at Simon & Schuster, a book about the improvement of education in American schools.
2015	*The Visit* released, which is self-produced by Shyamalan and seen as a return to form by many critics; debut of collaboration with micro-budget horror movie producer Jason Blum; first Season of *Wayward Pines* premieres on FOX.
2016	First music video clip *Rise Up* released for R&B singer Andra Day.
2017	*Split* released, which is a continuation of its own film *Unbreakable*; biggest box office hit since *Signs*.
2019	*Glass* released, which closes Shyamalan's Eastrail 177 trilogy after *Unbreakable* and *Split*; first season of *Servant* on Apple TV+ receives wide-ranging appraisal.
2021	*Old* released, first time that one of Shyamalan's thrillers is based on a different source material (the graphic novel *Sandcastle*); Shyamalan appointed in National Film Preservation Board.
2022	Becomes jury president of the Berlin International Film Festival.
2023	*Knock at the Cabin* released; the film is based on the novel *The Cabin at the End of the World* by Paul G. Tremblay.

Filmography

PRAYING WITH ANGER (1992)
101 minutes/color
Production Company: In-house production
Director: **M. Night Shyamalan**
Screenplay: **M. Night Shyamalan**
Producer: **M. Night Shyamalan**
Cinematography: Madhu Ambat
Editing: Frank Reynolds
Music: Edmund Choi
Starring: **M. Night Shyamalan**, Mike Muthu, Richa Ahuja Badami, Sushma Ahuja

WIDE AWAKE (1998)
88 minutes/color
Production Company: Woods Entertainment, Miramax Films
Director: **M. Night Shyamalan**
Screenplay: **M. Night Shyamalan**
Producer: Cathy Konrad, Cary Woods
Executive Producers: Bob Weinstein, Harvey Weinstein
Cinematography: Adam Holender
Editing: Andrew Mondshein
Casting: Avy Kaufman
Costume Design: Bridget Kelly
Music: Edmund Choi
Starring: Joseph Cross, Timothy Reifsnyder, Dana Delany, Denis Leary, Robert Loggia, Rosie O'Donnell, Camryn Manheim, Julia Stiles

SHE'S ALL THAT (1999)
95 minutes/color
Production Company: Tapestry Films, FilmMColony, Miramax
Director: Robert Iscove
Screenplay: R. Lee Fleming Jr., **M. Night Shyamalan**
Production: Peter Abrams, Richard N. Gladstein

Cinematography: Francis Kenny
Editing: Casey O. Rohrs
Music: Stewart Copeland
Cast: Freddie Prinze Jr, Rachael Leigh Cook, Matthew Lillard, Paul Walker, Kevin Pollak, Anna Paquin, Kieran Culkin, Usher

STUART LITTLE (1999)
107 minutes/color
Production Company: Columbia Pictures, Douglas Wick, Franklin/Waterman
Director: Rob Minkoff
Screenplay: **M. Night Shyamalan**, Greg Brooker
Producer: Jason Clark, Douglas Wick
Executive Producer: Jeff Franklin, Steve Waterman
Cinematography: Guillermo Navarro
Editing: Tom Finan
Casting: Debra Zane
Costume Design: Joanna Johnston
Music: Alan Silvestri
Starring: Michael J. Fox, Geena Davis, Hugh Laurie, Jonathan Lipnicki, Nathan Lane, Steve Zahn, Chazz Palminteri

THE SIXTH SENSE (1999)
107 minutes/color
Production Company: Hollywood Pictures, Spyglass Entertainment, the Kennedy/Marshall Company, Barry Mendel Pictures
Director: **M. Night Shyamalan**
Screenplay: **M. Night Shyamalan**
Producer: Kathleen Kennedy, Frank Marshall, Barry Mendel
Executive Producer: Sam Mercer
Cinematography: Tak Fujimoto
Editing: Andrew Mondshein
Casting: Avy Kaufman
Costume Design: Joanna Johnston
Music by James Newton Howard
Starring: Bruce Willis, Haley Joel Osment, Toni Collette, Olivia Williams, Trevor Morgan, Donnie Wahlberg, Mischa Barton, Greg Wood

UNBREAKABLE (2000)
106 minutes/color
Production Company: Touchstone Pictures, Blinding Edge Pictures

Director: **M. Night Shyamalan**
Screenplay: **M. Night Shyamalan**
Producer: **M. Night Shyamalan**, Sam Mercer, Barry Mendel
Executive Producer: Gary Barber, Roger Birnbaum
Cinematography: Eduardo Serra
Editing: Dylan Tichenor
Casting: Douglas Aibel
Costume Design: Joanna Johnston
Music: James Newton Howard
Starring: Bruce Willis, Samuel L. Jackson, Robin Wright, Spencer Treat Clark, Charlayne Woodard, Eamonn Walker, Leslie Stefanson

SIGNS (2002)
106 minutes/color
Production Company: Touchstone Pictures, Blinding Edge Pictures, the Kennedy/Marshall Company
Director: **M. Night Shyamalan**
Screenplay: **M. Night Shyamalan**
Producer: Sam Mercer, Frank Marshall, **M. Night Shyamalan**
Executive Producer: Kathleen Kennedy
Cinematography: Tak Fujimoto
Editing: Barbara Tulliver
Casting: Douglas Aibel
Costume Design: Ann Roth
Music: James Newton Howard
Starring: Mel Gibson, Joaquin Phoenix, Rory Culkin, Abigail Breslin, Cherry Jones, Patricia Kalember, **M. Night Shyamalan**

THE BURIED SECRET OF M. NIGHT SHYAMALAN (fake documentary for Syfy) (2004)
45 minutes
Production Company: Blinding Edge Pictures
Director: Nathaniel Kahn
Screenplay: Melissa Foster
Producer: Geoff Garrett, Callum Greene
Cinematography: Robert Richman
Editing: Brad Fuller, Geraldine Peroni
Music: Jeff Beal
Cast: Billy Arrowood, Adrien Brody, Johnny Depp, Deepak Chopra, **M. Night Shyamalan**

THE VILLAGE (2004)
108 minutes/color
Production Company: Touchstone Pictures, Blinding Edge Pictures, Scott Rudin Productions
Director: **M. Night Shyamalan**
Screenplay: **M. Night Shyamalan**
Producer: Scott Rudin, Sam Mercer, **M. Night Shyamalan**
Executive Producer: Jose L. Rodriguez
Cinematography: Roger Deakins
Editing: Christopher Tellefsen
Casting: Douglas Aibel
Costume Design: Ann Roth
Music: James Newton Howard
Starring: Bryce Dallas Howard, Joaquin Phoenix, Adrien Brody, William Hurt, Sigourney Weaver, Brendan Gleeson, Cherry Jones, Celia Weston, Frank Collison, Judy Greer, Michael Pitt, Jesse Eisenberg

TIME TO DREAM (commercial for American Express) (2006)
2 minutes/color
Director: **M. Night Shyamalan**
Concept: Ogilvy & Mather New York
Producer: Blinding Edge Pictures
Executive Producer: Sam Mercer, Jose Rodriguez
Cinematography: Christopher Doyle
Editing: Hank Corwin
Music: Paul Cantalone
Cast: **M. Night Shyamalan**

LADY IN THE WATER (2006)
110 minutes/color
Production Company: Warner Bros., Legendary Pictures, Blinding Edge Pictures
Director: **M. Night Shyamalan**
Screenplay: **M. Night Shyamalan**
Producer: Sam Mercer, **M. Night Shyamalan**
Executive Producer: Jose L. Rodriguez
Cinematography: Christopher Doyle
Editing: Barbara Tulliver
Casting: Douglas Aibel
Costume Design: Betsy Heimann

Music: James Newton Howard
Starring: Paul Giamatti, Bryce Dallas Howard, Jeffrey Wright, Bob Balaban, Sarita Choudhury, Freddy Rodriguez, Cindy Cheung, Bill Irwin, Mary Beth Hurt, Noah Gray-Cabey, **M. Night Shyamalan**

THE HAPPENING (2008)
91 minutes/color
Production Company: 20th Century Fox
Director: **M. Night Shyamalan**
Screenplay: **M. Night Shyamalan**
Producer: Sam Mercer, Barry Mendel, **M. Night Shyamalan**
Executive Producer: Gary Barber, Roger Birnbaum, Zarina Screwvala
Director of Photography: Tak Fujimoto
Editing: Conrad Buff IV
Casting: Douglas Aibel, Stephanie Holbrook
Costume Design: Betsy Heimann
Music: James Newton Howard
Starring: Mark Wahlberg, Zooey Deschanel, John Leguizamo, Ashlyn Sanchez, Betty Buckley, Spencer Breslin, Robert Bailey Jr., Frank Collison, Jeremy Strong

DEVIL (2010)
80 minutes/color
Production Company: Night Chronicles (Blinding Edge Pictures), Media Rights Capital
Director: John Erick Dowdle
Screenplay: **M. Night Shyamalan**, Brian Nelson
Producers: Sam Mercer, **M. Night Shyamalan**, Ashwin Rajan, John Rusk
Executive Producer: Trish Hofmann, Drew Dowdle
Director of Photography: Tak Fujimoto
Editing: Elliot Greenberg
Casting: Douglas Aibel, Debra Zane, Robin D. Cook
Costume Design: Erin Benach
Music: Fernando Velazquez
Starring: Chris Messina, Caroline Dhavernas, Bokeem, Woodbine, Logan Marshall-Green, Jenny O'Hara, Bojana Novakovic, Geoffrey Arend, Jacob Vargas, Matt Craven

THE LAST AIRBENDER (2010)
103 minutes/color

Production Company: Paramount Pictures, Nickelodeon Films, Blinding Edge Pictures, the Kennedy/Marshall Company
Director: **M. Night Shyamalan**
Screenplay: **M. Night Shyamalan**
Producer: Sam Mercer, Frank Marshall, **M. Night Shyamalan**
Executive Producers: Kathleen Kennedy, Bryan Konietzko, Michael Dante DiMartino, Scott Aversano
Director of Photography: Andrew Lesnie
Editing: Conrad Buff IV
Casting: Douglas Aibel
Costume Design: Judianna Makovsky
Music: James Newton Howard
Starring: Noah Ringer, Dev Patel, Nicola Peltz, Jackson Rathbone, Shaun Toub, Asaif Mandivi, Cliff Curtis, Seychelle Gabriel, Francis Guinan

AFTER EARTH (2013)
100 minutes/color
Production Company: Columbia Pictures, Blinding Edge Pictures, Overbrook Entertainment, Relativity Media
Director: **M. Night Shyamalan**
Screenplay: **M. Night Shyamalan**, Gary Whitta
Producers: James Lassiter, Jada Pinkett Smith, Caleeb Pinkett, Will Smith, **M. Night Shyamalan**
Executive Producer: E. Bennett Walsh
Director of Photography: Peter Suschitzky
Editing: Steven Rosenblum
Casting: Douglas Aibel
Costume Design: Amy Westcott
Music: James Newton Howard
Starring: Jaden Smith, Will Smith, Sophie Okonedo, Zoe Kravitz, Glenn Morshower, Kristofer Hivju

WAYWARD PINES (2015–2016)
20 episodes, 2 seasons, 40 minutes
Production Company: Blinding Edge Pictures, De Line Pictures, FX Productions, 20th Century Fox Television, Olive Entertainment
Directors: **M. Night Shyamalan**, Zal Batmanglij, James Foley, Tim Hunter, Nimród Antal, etc.
Screenplay: Blake Crouch, Chad Hodge, Edward Ricourt
Producers: Donald De Line, Shawn Williamson

Executive Producers: Chad Hodge, **M. Night Shyamalan**, Blake Crouch, Ashwin Rajan
Director of Photography: Jim Denault, Gregory Middleton, Amy Vincent
Editing: Doc Crotzer, Leo Trombetta, Michael Ruscio, John Axness, Glenn Farr, Elizabeth King
Casting: David Rubin
Music: Charlie Clouser
Starring: Toby Jones, Siobhan Fallon Hogan, Hope Davis, Shannyn Sossamon, Carla Gugino, Melissa Leo, Matt Dillon, Jason Patric, Nimrat Kaur, Djimon Hounsou, Terrence Howard

THE VISIT (2015)
94 minutes/color
Production Company: Blinding Edge Pictures, Blumhouse
Director: **M. Night Shyamalan**
Screenplay: **M. Night Shyamalan**
Producer: Jason Blum, Marc Bienstock, **M. Night Shyamalan**
Executive Producer: Ashwin Rajan, Steven Schneider
Cinematography: Maryse Alberti
Editing: Luke Ciarrocchi
Casting: Douglas Aibel
Costume Design: Amy Westcott
Starring: Olivia DeJonge, Ed Oxenbould, Deanna Dunagan, Peter McRobbie, Kathryn Hahn, Celia Keenan-Bolger

RISE UP (music video for Andra Day, album *Cheers to the Fall*) (2016)
4 minutes
Production Company: Collaboration Factory
Director: **M. Night Shyamalan**
Screenplay: Andra Day
Producer: Thom Fennessey, Ashwin Rajan
Executive Producer: Ashwin Rajan, Thom Fennessey
Cinematography: Kyle Rudolph
Editing: Luke Ciarrocchi
Music: Andra Day
Cast: Gregory Mozgala, Bisserat Tseggai, Mark Garcia

SPLIT (2016)
117 minutes/color
Production Company: Blinding Edge Pictures, Blumhouse, Universal Pictures

Director: **M. Night Shyamalan**
Screenplay: **M. Night Shyamalan**
Producer: Jason Blum, Marc Bienstock, **M. Night Shyamalan**
Executive Producer: Ashwin Rajan, Steven Schneider
Cinematography: Mike Gioulakis
Editing: Luke Ciarrocchi
Casting: Douglas Aibel
Costume Design: Paco Delgado
Music: West Dylan Thordson
Starring: James McAvoy, Anya Taylor-Joy, Betty Buckley, Haley Lu Richardson, Jessica Sula, Izzie Coffey, Brad William Henke, Sebastian Arcelus

GLASS (2019)
129 minutes/color
Production Company: Blinding Edge Pictures, Blumhouse, Buena Vista International, Universal Pictures
Director: **M. Night Shyamalan**
Screenplay: **M. Night Shyamalan**
Producer: Jason Blum, Marc Bienstock, **M. Night Shyamalan**, Ashwin Rajan
Executive Producer: Gary Barber, Roger Birnbaum, Steven Schneider
Director of Photography: Mike Gioulakis
Editing: Luke Ciarrocchi
Casting: Douglas Aibel
Costume Design: Paco Delgado
Music: West Dylan Thordson
Starring: James McAvoy, Bruce Willis, Samuel L. Jackson, Anya Taylor-Joy, Sarah Paulson, Spencer Treat Clark, Charlayne Woodard, Luke Kirby, Adam David Thompson

SERVANT (2019–2023)
40 episodes, 4 seasons, 30 minutes
Production Company: Blinding Edge Pictures
Directors: **M. Night Shyamalan**, Lisa Brühlmann, Isabella Eklöf, Julia Ducournau, Daniel Sackheim, Ishana Shyamalan, etc.
Screenplay: Tony Basgallop, Nina Braddock, etc.
Producer: Patrick Markey, Larissa Michel
Executive Producer: **M. Night Shyamalan**, Ashwin Rajan, Steve Tisch, Jason Blumenthal, Todd Black, Tony Basgallop
Cinematography: Mike Gioulakis, Marshall Adams, Jarin Blascke, etc.
Editing: Brett M. Reed, Harvey Rosenstock, Luke Doolan, etc.

Casting: Douglas Aibel, Stephanie Holbrook, Diane Heery, etc.
Costume: Caroline Duncan
Music: Trevor Gureckis
Starring: Lauren Ambrose, Rupert Grint, Toby Kebbell, Narci Regina, Jeffrey Mowery, Nell Tiger Free

OLD (2021)
109 minutes/color
Production Company: Blinding Edge Pictures, Universal Pictures
Director: **M. Night Shyamalan**
Screenplay: **M. Night Shyamalan**
Producer: Marc Bienstock, **M. Night Shyamalan**, Ashwin Rajan
Executive Producer: Steven Schneider
Cinematography: Mike Gioulakis
Editing: Brett M. Reed
Casting: Douglas Aibel
Costume Design: Caroline Duncan
Music: Trevor Gureckis
Starring: Eliza Scanlen, Abbey Lee, Rufus Sewell, Gael Garcia Bernal, Alex Wolff, Thomas McKenzie, Embeth Davidtz, Ken Leung, Vicky Krieps, Emun Elliott, Nikki Amuka-Bird, Aaron Pierre, **M. Night Shyamalan**

KNOCK AT THE CABIN (2023)
100 minutes/color
Production Company: Blinding Edge Pictures, Universal Pictures
Director: **M. Night Shyamalan**
Screenplay: **M. Night Shyamalan**, Steve Desmond, Michael Sherman
Producer: Marc Bienstock, **M. Night Shyamalan**, Ashwin Rajan
Executive Producer: Steven Schneider, Ashley Fox
Cinematography: Jarin Blaschke, Lowell A. Meyer
Editing: Noemi Katharina Preiswerk
Casting: Douglas Aibel
Costume Design: Caroline Duncan
Music: Herdis Stefánsdóttir
Starring: Jonathan Groff, Dave Bautista, Rupert Grint, Nikki Amuka-Bird, Ben Aldrige, Abby Quinn, William Ragsdale, Kristen Cui

M. Night Shyamalan: Interviews

Shyamalan's Indian Summer

Anne Thompson / 1993

From *LA Weekly* (April 1, 1993). Reprinted by permission of *LA Weekly*.

M. Night Shyamalan didn't follow through on a trip he'd planned to this February's American Film Market to help promote his first movie, *Praying with Anger*; instead, he was sidetracked into a marriage and a Mazatlán honeymoon. The business of screening and selling the film, which began at the Toronto Film Festival and continued at the Berlin Film Festival market, went on without him.

On the horn from Mexico, the twenty-two-year-old NYU graduate—who wrote, financed, produced, directed and starred in *Praying with Anger*, which he shot against all odds in Madras, India—sounded cheery. Last fall, the just-completed film was accepted by the Toronto Film Festival and later shown at the "First Look" series in New York, which helped Shyamalan land a distribution deal with small distributor Northern Arts and foreign sales company Unapix Films. They will open the film in New York and in Shyamalan's hometown, Philadelphia, on April 7.

While Shyamalan tends to succumb to the melodramatic self-promotion that characterizes so many young filmmakers, he feels generally threatened by Robert Rodriguez's *El Mariachi*. "That's my Achilles' heel," he blurts out, all too aware that the release of *El Mariachi* has a much better back story, to which many journalists have eagerly responded (how can you beat a $7,000 negative?), and that Rodriguez, who also went to film school (at the University of Texas, Austin), has made a far more commercial genre picture. Columbia Pictures, after all, was willing to spend $1 million to blow the movie up to 35mm and release it in major US cities.

Praying with Anger, on the other hand, it's a sensitive coming-of-age drama laden with emotion. "How many Hollywood films are made without a gun, without violence or sex?" asks Shyamalan, whose favorite filmmakers are Oliver Stone, John McTiernan and Rob Reiner. "They'll hire you to make a new action film, but not *Moonstruck*. *Praying with Anger* is definitely not a 'vehicle.' If there is a merit scale for young filmmakers, I don't fit on that scale."

Shyamalan assembled the ingredients for *Praying with Anger* much the way fellow NYU film grad Spike Lee did with 1986's *She's Gotta Have It*—from the shards of a shattered film deal. Shyamalan had been writing one script after another while in school, and when his second project, which was set to go for $1.5 million, fell apart, he decided to keep the investors he had lined up (he insists that they weren't family members) and make a $750,000 movie instead.

After graduating from NYU in May 1991, Shyamalan traveled to Madras, one of India's major film centers and his parents' hometown, and from that scouting trip cobbled together a screenplay featuring an American character very much like himself, a college student seeing India for the first time in the wake of his father's death. "I was careful to write a role I could handle," he admits, "from the perspective of someone who doesn't know anything about India."

Shyamalan hired an Indian cast and crew, and then the last-minute stroke of luck, landed one of India's top cinematographers, Madhu Ambat. Shyamalan credited his parents, who are doctors, as associate producers because, he says, "They put in a lot of time. We needed police to control the crowds. We included the cost of greasing people's palms in the budget."

After cutting the picture back in New York, Shyamalan submitted it to the Toronto Film Festival—very late, but it was accepted, and the young director began blanketing Toronto with fliers and talking up the press. One producers' representative recalls a rather breathless letter in which Shyamalan touted how well the film had played in its first preview. (It did grab an upbeat *Variety* review out of Toronto, and several small distributors expressed interest.)

Shyamalan eventually signed with an ICM agent and a lawyer, and suffered the harrowing experience of screening *Praying with Anger* for the jaded New York film-industry crowd that attends the monthly "First Look" series of the new films for would-be distributors and exhibitors at Tribeca Film Center. "New Yorkers may not hoot and holler," says Shyamalan, "but we closed the deal with Northern Arts several days after the "First Look" screening." Northern Arts is a mom-and-pop operation, and this will be their No. 1 film.

At February's American Film Market, Unapix president David M. Fox continued to discuss distribution deals for Germany, Italy, England and Australia. The Cannes market, in May, will immediately follow the US initial engagements. "*Praying with Anger* has no stars and no identifiable genre," admits Fox, "but it had a direct emotional impact on me. Film intellectuals don't like the film, which I think has the potential to reach a mass audience. I'm putting up $450,000 in P&A [prints and ads], the most Northern Arts has ever had."

Shyamalan eventually turned up in LA to talk his next deal, *Black Sheep*, about an Indian boy in an Episcopal prep school. "I'm going to get to do what I want," says Shyamalan, "without compromise." Lots of luck.

Dawn of Night

Carrie Rickey / 1998

From the *Philadelphia Inquirer* (March 8, 1998). Reprinted by permission of Even Benn, Director of Special Projects, the *Philadelphia Inquirer*, and Carrie Rickey.

Over his thirty years in the business, the Kodak guy thought he'd heard it all. He'd sold film stock to the Scorsese clones and the Spielberg wannabes. He'd met with film students ready to max out their credit cards and frugal visionaries wanting to buy cheap film left over from big-budget movies. He'd answered technical questions about emulsions and practical questions about discounts.

Never before, though, had the Kodak guy met anyone like this kid in blue jeans who wanted to know which film stock works best for creating emotional texture. "To understand how the stock is used for storytelling means, you should talk to your director of photography," Bob Strickland, Kodak account executive, gently advises the young filmmaker in a cramped Manhattan office.

Yet the director, M. Night Shyamalan, will not be denied. He apologizes if this sounds naive, but he wants Strickland's thoughts about the emotional spectrum as well as the color spectrum of a given film stock precisely in order to better communicate with his director of photography. Forgive me, Shyamalan says disarmingly, if the only way of getting smarter is to ask some dumb questions.

To determine whether Shyamalan would better be served by an account exec for low-cost features, Strickland casually asks, "How big a budget do you have?"

"Just under $30 million," Shyamalan replies. Strickland's jaw doesn't exactly drop, but it does visibly twitch.

M. Night Shyamalan (SHAH-ma-lawn) is twenty-seven. While you may not have heard of the Philadelphia filmmaker who grew up in Penn Valley and now lives with his wife, Bhavna, and their infant daughter, Saleka, in Wayne, understand that he is the talk of Hollywood. Scratch that. He is the buzz of the entertainment biz on both coasts.

Over drinks at the Polo Lounge, tongues are wagging about that Shyamalan kid who sold his screenplay, *The Sixth Sense*, to Disney's Hollywood Films for

$3 million on the condition that he direct. Bruce Willis signed to star in *Sense*, described as "a cross between *The Exorcist* and *Ordinary People*," a mood piece about a psychologist and his ten-year-old patient.

Shyamalan? Isn't he the one who wrote the script *Labor of Love* that Wolfgang Petersen (*Air Force One*) plans to direct for Fox? Isn't he the kid who did the *Stuart Little* rewrite that Rob Minkoff (*The Lion King*) is scheduled to make for Columbia?

Anticipation is high for *Wide Awake*, Shyamalan's winning comedy about a ten-year-old who literally and figuratively finds God. The film was shot on the Main Line two years ago and is set to open later this month.

But what really has the wags wagging is that the Philadelphia newcomer is so resistant to going Hollywood that he is bringing Hollywood to Philadelphia. Like *Wide Awake*, *The Sixth Sense* will be made in Shyamalan's hometown.

While established screenwriters such as Joe Eszterhas have sold spec scenarios (remember *Basic Instinct*?) for the big $3.0, no relative unknown has ever before commanded such a fee.

"The amazing thing about this sale, though," says Peter Benedek, Shyamalan's agent (and Curtis Hanson's and the Coen brothers' agent), "was that we didn't just sell a script, we sold a 'go' movie. I can't think of another example of a script being sold that didn't need further development before it went into production."

Those who know Shyamalan well do not talk in showbiz terms about the unprecedented money and power he has amassed at such a young age. They talk in terms of soul and heart. They marvel that *Wide Awake*, a movie costarring Rosie O'Donnell as a nun, a movie universal in its themes of spiritual doubt but so pro-Catholic that the archdiocese could use it as a recruiting film, happens to have been made by a practicing Hindu.

Manoj Night Shyamalan was born in Pondicherry, India, southwest of Madras, on August 6, 1970. His mother, Jayalakshmi, an obstetrician, and his father, Nelliate, a cardiologist, met in medical school in India before emigrating to Philadelphia in the 1960s. They returned to their homeland for the birth of their second child and only son. (Daughter Veena was born in 1964.) They called him Manoj, one of the names for the Hindu deity Krishna. You may call him by his middle name, however, for although he is an Indian son, he is also an American guy.

His parents worked long hours, until 8 p.m. After school at Waldron Academy (now Waldron Mercy, where much of *Wide Awake* was filmed), Night looked forward to coming home to a parent-free house. Once homework was done came Pretend Time, when earthquakes shook Penn Valley and galleons rode the Main Line's high seas. "The pillows on the sofa were boulders protecting me from a flood. The sofa was a boat on the stormy sea," Shyamalan recalls of his earliest adventure scenarios. "I didn't enjoy being the only Indian kid—and the smallest kid—in school," he replies. Although he is now a muscular 5-foot-11, when Shyamalan left Waldron in eighth grade, he stood barely 5 feet on a spindly, eighty-four-pound frame. "I feel fondly about Catholic school. I was a timid kid, the oversheltering was good for me. It gave structure."

As a family, the Shyamalans religiously attended the Flower Show every spring. Summer meant July 4 fireworks at Penn's Landing. Night's father, an American history buff, ritually took the family to historic sites such as Independence Hall.

By the time he entered Episcopal Academy in ninth grade, Shyamalan was being groomed for a career as a physician, like his parents and twelve of his aunts and uncles. But Night was writing screenplays. He was already a veteran director, having made home movies since the age of ten. "My Dad had a Bell & Howell 8mm movie camera that I started playing around with," he recalls. "Just silly things, like a person walking through the woods getting chased."

Shyamalan spent entire weekends with the camera. He found stories hidden in the neighborhood landscapes. He played with tempo, with editing, with point-of-view. Decades before his encounter with the Kodak guy, he was trying to find technical means of expressing the emotional. He was not a mall rat. He did not go to video arcades. "I am an Indian son. Indian sons don't hang out," he says. The rare occasions he went out without his family were to the movies. At seven, he saw *Star Wars* at the City Line Theater. At eleven, it was *Raiders of the Lost Ark* at the Narberth. "I went grudgingly with a friend. Who wanted to see some guys digging up old stuff?" he remembers. "*Raiders* was the singular greatest experience of my life to that point. It gave me the same feeling I had when I played pretend."

The following year he saw *E.T.* and *Gandhi*, loving the former for its supernatural awe, the latter for its spiritual drama. On Oscar night when both movies were competing for Best Picture, young Night prayed for a tie. However apocryphal this sounds, Shyamalan's screenplays *Wide Awake* and *The Sixth Sense* combine themes from both films, the respect for boyish wonder and reverence for mature faith.

"At first, there was a total disconnect between what I was doing at home on weekends and the movies I saw in theaters," he says. But by the time he was at Episcopal and a National Merit Scholar, highly regarded as an early-decision candidate for the premed program at Penn, Shyamalan started thinking that maybe what Spielberg did wasn't that different from what he did in his spare time. It slowly dawned on Night that he wanted to attend New York University's undergraduate film program. He told his folks that he was having second thoughts about going into the family business. "My parents aren't the type to scream and yell," he reflects. "They get real quiet, which is worse."

For the Drs. Shyamalan, medical school was a sure thing leading to a secure future; film school was a gamble that might lead to flipping burgers. Night, always goal-oriented, had to justify his parents' expectations. "Their standards for me were the highest. If I didn't make the best grades, if I didn't win the full scholarship, if I didn't get the $3 million for the screenplay, the question would inevitably be, 'Well, why not?'"

"My biggest fear in life," Shyamalan says bluntly, "is to be average."

Shyamalan enrolled at New York University and met Bhavna, a psychology student from India, now a doctoral candidate at Bryn Mawr. "I was immediately in love," he says. "I told my roommate, 'Just met the perfect girl for me, but she's dating someone else.'"

Not long after, a group of students in the NYU Indian community made a date to see *Working Girl*, but only Night and Bhavna showed up. "After the movie, when we went walking and held hands, we felt some chemistry," he says. "Her parents were on the verge of engaging her, and although it wasn't completely conscious, I had to preempt her parents' plans."

More conscious was the need to define himself artistically, which is a lot to ask of an eighteen-year-old with limited life experience. To develop his aesthetic, he took courses outside the film school: lit, psych. He was less interested in exploring visual styles than character and behavior. The department's chief requirement was the completion of one screenplay by graduation. Shyamalan wrote several, including *Wide Awake*. While most of his fellow students were completing the screenplay requirement, Shyamalan was negotiating with investors to make *Wide Awake* for $1.5 million.

"Since your diploma from film school means nothing, I had this self-imposed pressure," he recalls. "I had to prove to my parents and myself that this is what I was meant to do. I had the nerve of a novice." He traveled through the independent film community looking for money and asked his uncle's friends if they wanted to invest in a movie. The deal crashed. But out of its ashes came the idea for his first feature, *Praying with Anger*, a $750,000 epic starring Shyamalan as an Indian American youth who returns to Madras to explore his roots. The money came from some of the *Wide Awake* investors and some others in India.

A montage of Shyamalan's life since 1991:

- 1992: Goes to Madras to shoot *Praying with Anger*; receives $60,000 fee.
- 1993: Marries Bhavna at a Fort Washington country club; pays for wedding with part of his salary. *Anger* released in May, lukewarm *Inquirer* review effectively kills national distribution.
- 1993–94: Writes *Labor of Love*, about a widower's act of dedication to his late wife.
- 1994: Bidding war for *Labor of Love* nets $750,000 and guarantees Shyamalan the right to direct; Fox reneges on directing clause. With proceeds from screenplay sale buys first car.

- 1995: Sells *Wide Awake* to Miramax "for nothing" ($250,000!), on the condition that he direct—in Philadelphia.
- 1996: Casts Robert Loggia, Rosie O'Donnell and Denis Leary in *Wide Awake*. Daughter Saleka (Sanskrit for "to do things in the right way") born.
- 1997: By day, works on rewrite of script of E. B. White's *Stuart Little*. Paid $600,000 (and uses a portion to pay cash for house in Wayne). By night, writes original screenplay for *The Sixth Sense*. Bidding war nets $3 million and guarantee to direct. Uses fraction of that payment to buy two lots in Conshohocken to build dream house. Bruce Willis signs to make *Sense*.

That's one way to synopsize the last six years, Shyamalan says in late January on the Pennsylvania Turnpike, behind the wheel of his Rodeo, munching on an Egg McMuffin. He's New York–bound to meet with the Kodak guy, Miramax honcho Harvey Weinstein and a costume designer.

A different way to recap—the Hollywood way—would be to compare the budgets of his three films. *Praying with Anger*: $750,000. *Wide Awake*: $7 million. *The Sixth Sense*: $30 million.

Yet a third way to tell the story—the Shyamalan way—would be to conduct an emotional analysis rather than a cost analysis. The armfuls of accomplishments and handful of setbacks do not account for his depression in the wake of *Praying with Anger*. Nor do they account for his disillusion after *Wide Awake*, an emotionally depleting shoot during which he had to fire his cinematographer and friend. "A lot of stress—emotional, financial, everything," he says. Maybe it was too soul-destroying to direct. Maybe he would just concentrate on screenwriting.

Writing *The Sixth Sense* restored him. It reminded him of the highs he enjoyed as a director, like the time in 1992 when he premiered *Praying with Anger* at the Toronto Film Festival to enthusiastic audience response and reviews. There he was in Toronto, just twenty-two, sitting on a panel with Quentin Tarantino, Mr. Cool Reservoir Dogs, and Baz Luhrmann, Mr. Cool Strictly Ballroom, and Roberto Rodriguez, Señor Cool El Mariachi.

Shyamalan—who still saw himself as this scrawny kid and the only Indian— admits that he was never cool, "not in school, not now," not even in his dreams. So when a Polish woman stood up and hectored Tarantino, Luhrmann and Rodriguez, he was startled. Pointing at Shyamalan she said, "You have a lot to learn from him." Huh, wondered the hipsters. "His movie has no cursing, no smoking." Recalls Shyamalan, with a laugh: "It was as if Mom had walked into the locker room."

Why doesn't Shyamalan live in New York or Los Angeles, like 95 percent of Hollywood filmmakers? Shyamalan considers the question as he steers his Rodeo into the Lincoln Tunnel. "LA is an unnatural place for me. I wouldn't want to write about women with silicone implants or where to eat lunch," he says. "Philadelphia inspires me. What inspires me is how normal it is. In Philadelphia, I have direct access to my childhood feelings."

Out in Hollywood, though, some darkly predict that living outside the NY/LA bubble means Shyamalan will not derive the benefits of its nurturing and protection. "Because Night generates his own material and because he's so supremely talented, it doesn't matter where he lives," says his Beverly Hills–based agent Benedek, who thinks the Philadelphia angle actually "may even add to Night's mystique, like John Hughes never leaving Chicago."

Miramax chief Weinstein, who launched Tarantino and Kevin Smith (*Clerks*), says "Night Shyamalan is like Frank Capra. Night has great humanity." When the starmaker first read *Wide Awake*, "I heard my mother's voice saying to me, make this movie."

Between meetings with the Kodak guy and costume designer Suzy Benzinger, whose credits include Woody Allen's *Deconstructing Harry* and *Celebrity*, Shyamalan talks about which filmmakers he most admires.

"Steven Zaillian," he says, "because of *Searching for Bobby Fischer*, which he wrote and directed, and for the screenplays for *Schindler's List* and *Awakenings*. His body of work is quite eloquent." Shyamalan still defines himself more as a storyteller rather than as a visual artist. He's more like the emerging group of unironic, uncool types like Matt Damon and Ben Affleck (*Good Will Hunting*) and Jake Kasdan (*Zero Effect*) than Tarantino. But he's loath to criticize anyone.

"I'm like Gandhi, I only see good in movies," he says. "Quentin's the best at making substance out of surface," Shyamalan says. "He's an amazing technician." (Since tact doesn't get you very far in Hollywood, maybe it's good that he's not moving there.)

"I cast rough-edged people like Robert Loggia and Bruce Willis to deliver my lines, because I'm soft," he explains. Whether this softness is part of an emerging generational trend, what Weinstein calls "romantics dealing with the issues around growing up," or simply counterprogramming, Shyamalan does not know. What he does know is that "I want to make personal films that people will line up around the world to see."

Of all the fears plaguing a young filmmaker, looming perhaps larger than the fear of failure is the fear of disrespect. Here is Shyamalan, eager beaver, facing jaded technicians, producers and moguls who are sometimes, shall we say, patronizing?

"There's this thing I call the Yoda Syndrome," Shyamalan says, preparing for yet another encounter with someone at least a decade his senior. "Some people I work with get that Yoda thing in their voice. It's a condescending tone. I have to tell them, 'We're working on the same film, so now we're in the same place, we should be equals.'"

Karate gives him both an outlet for the frustrations and the discipline he craves. He is now a third-degree brown belt. Preparing for a meeting, he breathes deeply and his eyes get like tunnel-vision high beams. "There's this line in Zen philosophy: The beginner sees many possibilities," he says. "The expert sees few."

Almost everyone who knows Shyamalan remarks upon the man-child thing. "Here is this grown intellectual who still has his inner child," Weinstein marvels.

"I still think of myself as a little boy," admits the filmmaker whose ten-year-old heroes are both conventionally callow and startlingly wise. As a writer he does not project adult wisdom onto prepubescents; he focuses on that emotional (rather than biological) moment when boy becomes man but still retains that youthful élan.

At twenty-seven, Shyamalan is too old to be a prodigy. But listening to him, it's easy to think about reincarnation, about transmigration of spirit. Listening to him you think: Young blood, old soul.

Extrasensory Perception

Stephen Pizzello / 2000

From *American Cinematographer* (December 2000). Reprinted by permission of Stephen Pizzello and *American Cinematographer*.

Last year, when *The Sixth Sense* came out of nowhere to become the biggest box-office thriller of all time, grossing $650 million worldwide, director M. Night Shyamalan was thrust headlong into the industry spotlight. Like many previous filmmakers who had been anointed "young geniuses," the twenty-nine-year-old Shyamalan suddenly found himself shouldering the weight of great expectations.

Fortunately, Shyamalan, now at the ripe old age of thirty, was well prepared for cinematic success. Born in India and raised in the affluent Philadelphia suburb of Conshohocken, he made his first short film at age twelve using his father's 8mm camera. He wrote his first script at fifteen, and later attended film school at New York University. Intelligent, savvy and remarkably well versed in both film theory and practice, Shyamalan exudes ambition and boundless confidence; he even had the chutzpah to tell *Esquire* magazine that he thinks he's discovered the secret to making blockbuster movies. His theory, he told interviewer Michael D'Antonio, "explains why one film that seems great doesn't connect with the audience, but one that doesn't seem great can. Critics might not like it, but the audience does. Some writers or directors do it once, but by accident. The one guy who really knows it, as far as I can tell, is Spielberg, and he may be the only one."

Pressed to reveal this magic formula, Shyamalan demurred, noting that his undisclosed theory would be put to the test with *Unbreakable*, which does bear certain similarities to *The Sixth Sense*: it's a paranormal tale centering around a troubled family, it stars Bruce Willis, and it was scripted by the director himself. On this picture, however, Shyamalan worked with a different director of photography, Eduardo Serra, AFC, who was able to infuse the film with a new and distinctive visual style.

Although the narrative twists of *Unbreakable* were being kept under tight wraps, Shyamalan was gracious enough to offer *AC* some intriguing details about the film during a friendly and freewheeling phone call from his base of operations in Philadelphia.

Stephen Pizzello: What inspires you to dream up stories with paranormal themes?

M. Night Shyamalan: I don't have that as an agenda, but when I sit down to write a story, it just often has that sort of bent; if it doesn't, it feels more two-dimensional than I'd like the movie to be. Somehow, when I add that supernatural angle, a story becomes whole to me.

Pizzello: Where did you get the idea for *Unbreakable*?

Shyamalan: It came from a couple of different sources. I was actually working on an idea for another movie, which involved the sole survivor of a plane crash in which everybody else dies and he emerges unharmed. Eventually, the character has this realization about who he is. I told my wife about the story, and she said, "Wow, you really need to do that." It was just a beautiful, simple, powerful idea that I knew I could write a two-hour movie about.

Pizzello: Even though *Unbreakable* has a fantastic premise, the story never strays far from the family dynamic at its core. The same could be said about *The Sixth Sense*, so I'm assuming that the idea of family is close to your heart.

Shyamalan: You're right; on both movies, I've basically taken a humanistic approach to supernatural subject matter. I find that approach to be the most compelling entrée into supernatural material, and it's also the point of view that gets me the most personally invested in that type of story. If you come up with an idea that involves, say, fairies or some other fantastic subject, it can be hard to relate to. I try to find a way to bring those kinds of fictional subjects, which are beyond the norm, to viewers in real ways that they can relate to. I want to make the audience feel fear, wonder and excitement, and I think it's easier to do that if you use marriages, children and the family dynamic as your jumping-off point. My main goal when I'm writing is to create a movie that has both a strong plot and a strong central character—someone like, say, Cool Hand Luke. You can build a whole movie around a strong character, but it works even better if the story is supported by a plot that's equally strong.

Pizzello: Do you plan to continue writing your own scripts exclusively? Does that way of working make things easier for you as a director?

Shyamalan: Yes and yes; I don't know, maybe I'm not a good enough director to do someone else's script! It takes me a long time to hack out my ideas, and then figure out what's wonderful and not so wonderful about [them]. I also think a lot about the tones I want to bring out of the subject matter, the dialogue and the characters. I spend months on all of those considerations, and once I sell the screenplay I begin storyboarding and prepping like crazy. Only after all of that stuff is done do I feel confident that I can go to the set and deliver a movie. The last two times out, on *The Sixth Sense* and *Unbreakable*, I've felt that all of my massive preparation gave me a real advantage in the battle to accurately bring those visions to the screen.

Pizzello: Did the tremendous success of *The Sixth Sense* have any bearing on your approach to *Unbreakable*?

Shyamalan: Definitely—just as the failure of my first feature film, *Wide Awake* [1998], had an effect upon *The Sixth Sense* in terms of my directing and the lessons I'd learned. On *The Sixth Sense*, I learned a lot about what worked in the movie, what didn't work, and why the film had such a resonant effect on people. I developed theories about those factors, and I tried to bring some of those elements to *Unbreakable*, while still attempting to move forward and try new things.

Pizzello: What led you to choose Eduardo Serra to be your director of photography on *Unbreakable*? Did you feel that he could help you create a new or different visual style for this picture?

Shyamalan: Well, I wanted the movie to have a European look, and I was trying to find a cinematographer who could make things look dark—but not the kind of darkness you'd see in a low-budget movie. I didn't want the film to be heavily lit, and Eduardo uses a lot of natural light. He can also make things look very natural even when they *are* lit. I basically needed someone who was comfortable with the concept of low-light photography. A lot of the cinematography I see today has a slick, nonrealistic look that conflicts with my goals. I want people to feel that the hallway onscreen is *their* hallway, or that the kitchen is *their* kitchen. Their house probably isn't going to have blue lights in front of revolving fans, you know? That's just an effect. I want the audience to feel totally connected with the story, so I need a cinematographer who can create naturalistic images that have style. When I was gearing up on *Unbreakable*, I met a lot of cinematographers who could get a natural look, but not all of them could find the style that exists within the natural world. Eduardo has a wonderful, effortless style, and he can create images that are both eerie and beautiful. His images do involve meticulous work, of course, but they look effortless.

Pizzello: What did the two of you discuss in prep, and what kind of dynamic did you have on the set?

Shyamalan: Well, he and I hit it off the first time we spoke on the phone. We got along great, and the collaboration was just awesome. Eduardo's training, theories and thought patterns come from paintings, and that's a great way for us to connect—he can show me a painting and say, "See how the light hits their faces? This is the effect I want to go for, and this is what I think it means emotionally."

On any movie, I have very strong ideas about how I want the scenes to feel visually, so I came up with the shots and then Eduardo fine-tuned them and lit them. At the prep stage, I showed him the first set of storyboards, and we walked through every shot and every part of storyboards, and we walked through every shot and every part of the movie. He then came up with a color palette and a lighting arc that would gradually change the mood of the story. He brings artistry to an aspect of picture-making that could be mechanical.

Pizzello: Did you have any specific visual influences in terms of the film's look? Comic books factor into the storyline, so I'm wondering if you drew any inspiration from the graphic style of comics.

Shyamalan: Yes, but in a very subtle way that remained within the parameters of naturalism. For example, Eduardo's lighting slowly becomes darker and more dramatic over the course of the movie. By the last thirty minutes, the shadows are so extreme that you feel as if you're watching *The Silence of the Lambs* or something! Actually, I suppose that one of my primary influences for this picture was one of Eduardo's previous pictures, *The Wings of the Dove*. That film's imagery had the combination of richness and gentleness that I wanted for *Unbreakable*. It felt very real and beautiful without being "artsy-fartsy." I liked the idea of incorporating that type of artistry into the kind of big-budget, supernatural movie that I do. A lot of Hollywood movies rely on that slick look to get a response from the audience, but I feel you should have to earn it.

Pizzello: You've mentioned the use of color and lighting arcs over the course of the movie. What are the other main elements of the film's visual style?

Shyamalan: I wanted the scenes to have a monochromatic backdrop, so that the movie would have an almost black-and-white feel and specific elements would pop out of the frame. That was a very meticulous strategy that affected the entire crew. A character couldn't just walk through the frame, he or she had to be dressed appropriately, the background had to be just right, and every car that moved through the frame had to be very specific.

Pizzello: Eduardo also said that you like your camera moves to be motivated by emotion.

Shyamalan: When you're watching a movie, the camera is *you*, so it's important for a filmmaker to really understand what a pan or a tilt means. A pan is not just moving from right to left; it has a certain emotional value, just as a tilt or a zoom does. A dolly straight on is different from a dolly on an angle. I have my own beliefs about what [various] moves mean, and while working with Eduardo I would go through them and say, "These are the emotions that I want to convey, so what's the best way to get them?"

Pizzello: Can you give me a specific example from *Unbreakable*?

Shyamalan: Okay, let's talk about a dolly move in the movie. There's a moment when Bruce's character has to make a decision. He has all of the information he needs, and as he makes his decision, we dolly straight on, from a low angle, right up to him. If it were a different moment for the character—if, say, he didn't understand what was going on, and then suddenly got it—we'd have come at him from an angle, and we wouldn't have been in front of him until his big realization. The character would still be doing the same thing in each of these examples—standing still and looking upwards—but the two different camera moves I've described would convey two different ideas.

Pizzello: What emotion do you attach to the Steadicam or to handheld camerawork?

Shyamalan: I'm still devising my opinion about what emotion a Steadicam move represents, and I'm not yet comfortable with my own analysis. The Steadicam has that floating feel, and I want to make sure I understand it more fully before I use it extensively.

On the other hand, I have a very clear grasp of what a handheld move brings to a scene and what it means emotionally. There are all types of handheld shots, but I always try to get *good* handheld shots—the idea is to try to make it as steady as possible, because it's not going to be steady no matter what you do! If you try as best you can to make handheld footage steady, it creates the idea that there's no brace involved and that something could go wrong. It conveys to viewers, but not in too obvious a way, that I'm not going to let them feel comfortable, that I'm going to keep them uneasy during the scene. If someone's yelling at someone in a kitchen and the camera is handheld, you get the feeling that something very bad could happen, and that you shouldn't feel secure.

Pizzello: How do you feel about filmmakers who use wild camera movement for its own sake?

Shyamalan: Frankly, I think a lot of those filmmakers have no clue when it comes to camera movement. Even when they try stuff, they're just guessing or borrowing—they'll say something like, "Okay, let's try that move from Marty Scorsese's last movie, that was really cool." Obviously, some of my ideas about camera movement *do* come from other movies I've seen, but I've always tried to tailor the camera moves I use to the particular story I'm telling.

Pizzello: I assume that your philosophies about the emotions of camera movement also extend to nonmoving compositions as well.

Shyamalan: Definitely. In fact, on *Unbreakable* I said to Eduardo and the crew, "There are no medium shots in this movie, because that would mean that the character is feeling medium. And if he's feeling medium, I don't need to tell anyone about it, because that's boring. If the character is feeling medium, that's the moment when we'll cut away to the next scene, because I want him to feel high and low instead." On this movie, each scene involved a very specific approach. In general, I seem to prefer symmetrical compositions shot with wider lenses. I don't like things to be too wide, because I don't want things to get distorted. I basically find a symmetrical frame to be a bit unnerving; as a viewer, you can see so much, and it all looks so perfect, that you begin to feel a bit insecure. You're waiting for something to happen, and that's when I've got you—even though I haven't really *done* anything yet.

Pizzello: You've apparently incorporated that type of suspense mechanism into the film's train-crash sequence, because you never really show the crash itself. It's all about the *anticipation* of the crash.

Shyamalan: I wanted that sequence to go right up to the moment of the crash and then stop.

Later on, you see the repercussions of the crash, but to me it's much more intriguing to show the thirty-five seconds before the accident happens—to show what that thirty-fourth second really feels like. I wanted to stretch out those thirty-five seconds and make sure the viewers understood every beat. During the shoot, we initially kept the sequence going a bit longer in order to show the first few seconds after the crash, but I eventually decided that it was more powerful to stop just before the impact.

Pizzello: Eduardo also mentioned that you don't generally like to shoot a master and a lot of close-ups. Instead, you use more composed shots that are very carefully storyboarded.

Shyamalan: Well, there's hardly any coverage in this movie at all. The movie was shot to look the way it was originally planned. There was no other way to cut it, and there was no way to save the movie if it didn't work. It wasn't a case of, "Let's figure it out in the editing room." A ton of editing was done, but only with the intention of crystallizing the original vision. If we were dealing with a close-up of Bruce or Sam, that was all we had to represent that particular moment in the movie; we were never saying things like, "Well, let's try the mid-shot of Bruce and Sam instead." As a director, I find it important to take a stance and say, "I have this image in my head, and let's do everything we can to make it happen." I'd rather use the production time to realize that vision. I don't want to shoot a backup version—I want to spend every single minute of my time blocking and choreographing and working the camera to convey that original vision. And I have confidence that at least 90 percent of the time, that's going to be the right decision.

Pizzello: It sounds like a very controlled way of working. Do you allow much improvisation in terms of the acting?

Shyamalan: [*Laughing*] Not really.

Pizzello: I guess that means that you belong more to the Alfred Hitchcock school of directing.

Shyamalan: Yeah, I could walk you through one of my movies before we shoot it, and you'd be astonished at how close the original vision is to the finished film.

Pizzello: Have you found that actors will respond to that type of approach if your vision is strong enough?

Shyamalan: They'll respond to it if the *script* is strong enough. If the script has holes, and you ask them to stick to that specific blueprint, it can become a very tense situation. If the script has been worked on very carefully, to the point where it's watertight, then they're willing to go there. I think actors like it when a director says, "This is what we're going for, and this is how I'm going to do it. Everything else is up to you. There are a thousand choices to be made in the next three minutes as I roll the camera, so go for it. You don't have to worry about all of the other stuff, because I've got that covered." That opens up all of those wonderful nuances that actors can give you with their eyes, their gestures, and so on.

Of course, when we go to the set to block out a scene, I do leave room so we can adjust things for the actors if they feel uncomfortable. For example, if someone says to me, "I wish I wasn't sitting down," no problem—I can find a way around that. As we go through the scene, we can adjust the vision that's been planned for five months, but it's more about customizing that vision than rethinking it.

Pizzello: Given your penchant for control, do you prefer working in a studio or at real locations?

Shyamalan: It usually ends up being about 50–50. My first choice is to find a location where I can do the shots I've come up with, and where [the cinematographer] can do this lighting. Sometimes we'll find a location where we can do the camera move, but we can't light the scene properly. Eventually, it becomes very obvious which settings need to be built and which ones we need to find.

Pizzello: What was the most challenging aspect of *Unbreakable* from your perspective?

Shyamalan: [*Laughing*] All of it—the whole thing was very tiring and challenging. Unfortunately, I didn't make any of the scenes easy; I made it really hard for both the crew and myself. We shot the entire movie in continuity, and I made all of these demands, like my "no coverage" rule. It was a super-challenging shoot both creatively and technically, but for me it became a very cathartic experience to pull it off. A movie like this one cannot be made in a half-assed way; it requires total concentration and commitment from everyone involved.

Out of This World

Jeff Giles / 2002

From *Newsweek* (August 2002). Reprinted by permission of *Newsweek* and Jeff Giles.

Looking back, the moment I liked M. Night Shyamalan most was the moment he liked me least, and that was the moment when he said he'll never understand why people occasionally think he's cocky and I said, "Well, you *are* cocky—maybe *that's* why." This exchange took place in the back seat of a black SUV as Shyamalan's driver, Franny, ferried us out to the Philadelphia suburbs so I could see where the thirty-one-year-old writer-director went to high school. Shyamalan wanted to know what he'd said that sounded cocky. "See, we have to clear this up," he said. "I can't believe you think that. *Cocky?* Give me an example." I was regretting that I'd opened my mouth. I told him I'd have to think about it. "Oh, now you've got to *think about it*. You had the statement right there in your hand with nothing to back it up!" The SUV pulled into the Episcopal Academy, in Merion. Shyamalan and I ducked into an administrative building, and a woman named Meg Hollinger whisked down the stairs. She told me that Shyamalan was a wonderful role model for the students, that he came to speak with them and that what struck her most about him was his humility. Shyamalan grinned, shot me a look and said, "See!" When we headed back out the door to tour the campus, he put his hand on my shoulder, a gesture, I later discovered, he inherited from his father. "I'm sorry," he said, pleasantly. "You weren't finished with your belligerent accusations."

Relax, Night, I'm about to say that you're a filmmaker who matters. At twenty-eight, Shyamalan—whose last name is pronounced *Sha-ma-lon*—wrote and directed *The Sixth Sense*, which starred Bruce Willis as a psychologist and Haley Joel Osment as a trembling boy besieged by ghosts. That movie, of course, had a spectacular twist ending, and grossed nearly $700 million worldwide. More than that, though, *The Sixth Sense* proved that even in summertime moviegoers did not need to be pummeled or condescended to. As Mel Gibson puts it, "That one he did about the dead people—that was a phenomenally crafted movie.

Night's uncompromising in the way he tells a story. He doesn't spoon-feed, and he doesn't pander to anyone." Shyamalan's follow-up, the somber *Unbreakable*, misfired at the box office. But his latest offering, *Signs* with Gibson, is a welcome return to form.

Shyamalan is every bit the movie buff that the seventies' auteurs were. His idols are unapologetically pop, though: not Fellini, Bergman and Kurosawa, but Hitchcock, Lucas and Spielberg. The scares in *Signs* call Hitchcock to mind, but Shyamalan is more akin to the young Spielberg in his careful rippling of the heartstrings, his deft touch with child actors, his fascination with the middle-class American family and his desperate desire to keep pleasing the same demographic over and over: people between the ages of ten and one hundred.

Shyamalan is already Hollywood's highest-paid screenwriter. Disney gave him $5 million to write *Signs* and $7.5 million to direct. Now he's attempting to turn his name into a brand, like Spielberg, so that on opening weekend audiences will converge to see not a Mel Gibson or a Bruce Willis movie, per se, but an M. Night Shyamalan movie with Gibson or Willis *in it*. Says Marc H. Glick, the director's lawyer and earliest supporter, "Where we're headed is, 'Shyamalan' will open the film."

Cocky is, in fairness, too lazy a label to stick on someone who's widely liked, introspective and hellbent on self-improvement. "It's funny," says the director. "We were on the set of *Signs* once—we were deep in the shooting—and we did something, and I went, 'No, no, no, I was wrong.' And Mel hugs me and goes, 'You said you were wrong! I can't believe it!' And I'm like, 'What are you talking about? I'm always wrong!' I can't be unclear about how I want to make movies. But that doesn't mean I'm right. It just means I'm clear." Point taken. But Shyamalan is nothing if not unabashed. He is Hollywood's next great entertainer. And I'm thinking he knows it.

Signs is an unusually moving thriller about a former priest named Graham (Gibson) who lost his wife in tragic circumstances—and his faith immediately thereafter. Graham, his brother (Joaquin Phoenix) and his kids (Rory Culkin and Abigail Breslin) are holed up in their Pennsylvania farmhouse when crop circles suddenly materialize in the cornfields, the first volley in what appears to be an alien invasion. Like all of Shyamalan's movies, it is obsessed not just with the unknown, but with family, parenting and self-renewal, and shot through with the unmistakable admonition that we must draw whoever is near and dear to us even nearer. The director's mother had not yet seen *Signs* when I interviewed her for this story. She will love it. "I feel he should make the nice movies," says Jayalakshmi Shyamalan, a retired obstetrician. "The latest thing—sex and that sort of thing—I am not for it. But it is a different profession. He would turn around and say, 'Mommy, I didn't tell you how to deliver a baby.' We don't have any control over what he's going to write, but I feel it should be something nice which leaves a landmark on the people who see it. Maybe a little spirituality. That would be the greatest thing."

Shyamalan's career seems especially significant at the moment because Hollywood at large is patently not making the nice movies. Or at least the fresh ones. This summer has been a rush of franchise pictures based on preexisting concepts and characters. Of course, attendance is up 15 percent—and so is self-congratulation. Which means it's getting exponentially less likely that mainstream filmmakers will do anything as radical as sit down and try to, you know, think stuff up. *Signs* will have to fight to be No. 1 because its release is bracketed by two blockbusters borrowing James Bond's mojo: *Austin Powers in Goldmember* and *XXX*. The latter was set to open the same day as *Signs*, but the *XXX* folks opted against going head-to-head and moved back seven days. "They're scared to death, man," says Shyamalan. "They're absolutely terrified." That didn't sound cocky, did it? Just checking. "Night thrives on being the one original movie in a sea of sequels and derivative products," says Disney Studios chairman Richard Cook. "He loves the competition. I think that's part of what gets him going."

One morning in June, Shyamalan paces around a sound-mixing studio in midtown Manhattan. On screen, Gibson's character and his family stand shellshocked in their front hall, as booms and bangs and what sound like scuttling claws start filling every corner of the house. At a mixing desk facing the screen, sound editors "audition" a series of noises for a crucial thud at the front door. Shyamalan considers each option with what, to an outsider, seems like an extraordinarily discerning ear. He tells the editors he doesn't want some cheesy, generic boom. He tells them the characters will seem smarter if they're responding to subtler noises—and that the audience's ears won't be ruined for quieter effects to come. All the while, he teases his team to keep the energy up, at one point telling sound mixer Michael Semanick to do the opposite of whatever he did on *Attack of the Clones*. Semanick laughs, and says over his shoulder, "You don't want $245 million in five weeks?" Shyamalan grins and shakes his head. "I'm telling you, if you'd done a great movie, you'd have made four times as much as that."

For the record, the *Star Wars* franchise has always been close to Shyamalan's heart, and he hasn't actually seen *Clones* yet: "I'm just giving Michael s--t." Still, the director is obsessed with understanding why audiences do the things they do. "Last year was probably the worst year for movies for me since I've been alive," he says, after settling into a leather chair. "It was the worst. The quality of movies in general. We don't have to get into specifics. And what that creates is a starvation in the audience. And, ironically, what *that* creates is . . . If they know what they're getting—like a franchise, something established—the starvation says, 'I'll take that. I'll come in droves.'" *Signs* will have to earn the audience's trust. "People believe in honesty. They really do," says Shyamalan. "And integrity—all the way down to the choice of a sound effect."

He pauses and looks up at the screen, where Gibson's character is trying to calm his kids down by telling them the stories of their births. They are the stories of Shyamalan's own daughters, five and two, being born. "What will come across is something pure," he continues. "*Hopefully*. A voice. It will be the voice of a kid who was born in India and grew up in Philly. That's the only thing I have on the 'Scooby-Doos.'" Later in the week, with *Signs* minutes away from being finished, Shyamalan shoots baskets in a portable hoop in the mixing room, and jokes around some more. "Let's say I decided to do *Pokémon 5*—would you come?" he asks Semanick, brightly. "You wouldn't come?" He turns to his film editor, Barbara Tulliver. "If I did *Pokémon 5*, would you come? Come on! I could turn it into a metaphor for the human condition!"

Shyamalan was born with the name Manoj in Pondicherry, India, during one of his parents' trips back home to visit family. A few months later, the Shyamalans returned to the Philadelphia suburbs, where his father, Nelliate, was a cardiologist. The director remembers being small for his age, an enormously sensitive kid scared of—well, what have you got? Everything. His family was inseparable—even today, they greet each other with a flurry of hugs and kisses, though they live only five minutes apart on the Main Line—and his mother says that whenever young Manoj had to be alone she'd call him every thirty minutes. Shyamalan was raised Hindu but sent to a Roman Catholic grade school for the discipline. Yes, he was aware of being *different* and *other*, but his memories of growing up have more to do with basketball and *Raiders of the Lost Ark*. He began making his movies at ten or so. He used an 8mm camera. He'd have to plug it into a VCR and lug the whole mess around with an extension cord.

Though Shyamalan tends to be quite frank in interviews, he hesitates when he's asked something that might affect his loved ones, might encroach on their "shared history." When I ask him if he drank or dated in high school, he grins nervously. "Uh, yeah. Are you gonna tell my parents? Are you gonna write that and tell my parents?" Surely they know. "I don't think they do! You're gonna shock them. They're gonna have a heart attack!" Shyamalan is laughing now. He is tall and broad-shouldered, but he has a laugh that is so childlike it is almost a giggle. While Shyamalan was at New York University studying film, he fell hard for a fellow student named Bhavna, who's now getting a PhD in child psychology. He proposed to her not long afterward with a note in a fortune cookie in a Chinese restaurant. "She was like, 'This is so weird. *This* says . . .'" He was already on his knees.

Shyamalan's first feature was an independent movie called *Praying with Anger*, which grossed $7,000 and change at the box office in 1992. He shot the movie in India to save money, and actually starred, turning in an endearingly creaky performance as an American finding his roots. (These days, Shyamalan limits himself to cameos.) Because *Praying with Anger* contains not one but two star-crossed romances, I ask Shyamalan if Bhavna's parents objected to their marriage. He does not giggle. "I don't know how I can talk about that without bringing in her business and her family's business," he says. "That's a shared history." He elaborates a bit, saying that Bhavna's family was from the north of India and that his was from the south, and he was slightly younger. Those things are deal-breakers in India, of course. "But everything's cool now," he says. I ask him if he'd ever thought about giving up. "No, I'm not that kind of guy." Did she? "Probably." How did he persuade her not to? "I'm kinda hard to get off your back when I want something."

In 1994, Shyamalan wrote a script called *Labor of Love*. Fox, he says, offered him hundreds of thousands of dollars, assuring him he could also direct. Once he had sold it to them, it became clear that they'd just been yesing him to get the screenplay. "I cried. It killed me. It was a story about what I felt about first being married. It was pure. I said, 'You can't do this.' So they flew me out and I met with all the bigwigs in a room. I was wearing a pin-striped suit. My mom got me that suit so I wore it. Apparently, you don't wear suits in Hollywood. So I walked in looking like some high-school kid trying to get a job. Immediately, there were all these jokes about my suit. They're like, 'Yeah, we're gonna give *you* a $25 million movie.'" The film was never made. "I cursed it."

When Shyamalan *did* get a second feature off the ground, in 1996, things actually went far, far worse. *Wide Awake* is about a Catholic schoolboy whose grandfather's death sets him on a search for God. After Shyamalan edited the film, Miramax's famed cochairman, Harvey Weinstein, insisted that it be recut. Rosie O'Donnell, who plays a nun in the movie, intervened on Shyamalan's behalf. A meeting was set so that everybody could clarify his position. O'Donnell got the flu, and had to call in on the speakerphone. Weinstein was already put out with her because she'd just fired a friend of his from her TV show. "I said, 'Listen, Harvey, I don't want you to release it unless it's Night's version,'" O'Donnell remembers. "'He's the artist. You're just the guy who frames it and sells it.' Well, you know what? That didn't go over big. He started saying, 'Who do you think you are? You're just a f---ing talk-show host!' He went *off*. I was stunned. I thought he *knew* that he acquired the films and that the other people were the artists. I didn't think this was news to him. He said, 'Like you would f---ing know. You b---h! You c--t!'"

O'Donnell cried, and told Weinstein to shove it somewhere very specific. "Night called me afterwards, like, 'Oh my God, are you all right?'" she says.

"Thank God Harvey didn't crush him, because it takes a lot to stand up to that. I gotta tell you, it takes a lot to make me cry and he *totally* made me cry." O'Donnell says that to Weinstein's credit he later apologized, sending her jewelry and flowers. Asked to respond to all of the above, Weinstein sent NEWSWEEK a gentlemanly statement: "Night is an incredibly talented filmmaker, and it's unfortunate for us that we were unable to find a successful way to market *Wide Awake*. It's one of my great disappointments, since I loved the film. Thank God for DVD."

Shyamalan himself regards the *Wide Awake* fracas as a pivotal moment in his career. "Harvey's just the way the world is," he says. "If the movie was great and was going to make a lot of money, it would have gone very smoothly." The episode taught him that making uncommercial movies makes you vulnerable and that, as he puts it, "I never want to be weakened and victimized again." (At one point while Shyamalan was in the mixing room finishing *Signs*, he joked to his film editor, "Harvey called. He wants you to recut this." Somebody else piped up, "He's heading right over." Chuckling ensued.)

After *Wide Awake* grossed all of $300,000, Shyamalan reminded himself that it was blockbusters like *Raiders* that inspired him in the first place. "I think Night recognized that he has a very sensitive, sentimental streak in him," says Barry Mendel, who produced *The Sixth Sense* and *Unbreakable*, "and that he needs to juxtapose that with something darker, edgier and more commercial." Shyamalan began writing a supernatural thriller about a serial killer and a boy who sees dead people. It was lousy at first. A *Silence of the Lambs* rip-off. Then he started thinking about the kid. What if he was a really sensitive kid, a kid so empathetic that he even felt bad for ghosts? Shyamalan wrote some dialogue for a birthday party—a turning point, though it never made it to the screen—where the sensitive kid and a chubby kid are just sitting there, friendless and ostracized. The sensitive kid tells the chubby kid, "My mom said God made some of us different, knowing that it'd be hard. But he picked the people who would be different really carefully." Then the sensitive kid leans forward to the chubby kid: "God thinks we're strong."

When Shyamalan finished writing 1999's *The Sixth Sense*, he told his agents at the United Talent Agency that he had a screenplay for them to sell and that *he* was going to direct it. No matter what. And that the minimum bid was $1 million. No matter what. Says Mendel, "Night came out to LA and he bought himself a new pair of shoes, and he and Bhavna checked into the Four Seasons *determined* to have something great happen." Disney gave him $3 million. "I was only ten," says Haley Joel Osment, "but I could tell it was amazing writing."

On the day that Shyamalan's driver, Franny, drives us out to the Episcopal Academy, the director and I have our spat about whether he's cocky or not, and then we walk around campus in a funk trying to find somewhere cool to talk. We wind up in the chapel, which is empty and quiet except for a whispering air conditioner. I ask Shyamalan about 2000's *Unbreakable*, about the making of a superhero. The movie was his second with Bruce Willis, and it was so grave and slow that it seemed to suggest he'd become overconfident about his ability to hold an audience. Shyamalan is fiercely proud of *Unbreakable* and of its status as a cult favorite. Still, when he talks about it, it's clear that if he *was* arrogant before it opened—*Sixth Sense* had made the all-time box-office Top Ten, and he was quoted as saying it'd be cool if *Unbreakable* made it, too—his theories about movies and audiences took a beating when *The Grinch* clobbered him at the box office.

"When *The Grinch* took us, it really shocked me," he says. "It was such a great lesson for me. *Signs* could go out there and completely tank, I'm telling you. I couldn't believe what was happening. *The Grinch* became the phenomenon! They stole Thanksgiving!" By the time we leave his old school, Shyamalan seems chipper. His driver heads the wrong way down a one-way street and, from the back seat, the director says, "Franny! I'm gonna get *expelled.*"

The thing that broke *Unbreakable*, of course, was the ghost of *Sixth Sense*. "I think Night suffered from second-film syndrome," says Willis. "People wanted to say, 'This guy isn't the genius that everyone said he is.' I don't use that word casually, but I believe he has elements of genius in him—as a writer, as a storyteller and as a film director." When I ask Shyamalan about his expectations for *Signs*, he sounds grounded. Sort of. "I don't care about the box office," he says. "I care about the connection. I want it to be a phenomenon—a cultural phenomenon, where the audience feels some connection to this place, these people and what was being said here. That's *Jaws*, *E.T.*, *The Exorcist*. All those movies. They just *connected.*" I tell someone that Shyamalan has worked with that the director is hoping for a cultural phenomenon, and he laughs fondly: "In my opinion, just even saying that is stupid. As a tactic, you know? Keep that to yourself! That's a fine goal but by saying it you're sticking your chin out and saying, 'Punch me.' I think that Night—and this is an endearing quality—is not that savvy about how to promote himself. He definitely wears what he's thinking and feeling on his sleeve."

The morning I leave Philadelphia, Shyamalan's parents offer to drive me to the train. As the green, leafy Main Line darts past the windows—beautiful lawn after beautiful lawn after beautiful lawn—I ask why Manoj ever stopped calling himself Manoj. "You are pronouncing it so *well*," his mother says, sweetly. (It's *Ma-noge*.) She says that Shyamalan's teachers used to mangle it, so when he was a teenager he came up with Night. His father tells me that his son always felt a kinship with the Native Americans, and that the word resonated for them because the elders told their children stories around the fire in the evening and because you can see the universe only at night. Also, his father adds, "it was a good entertainment name." And there are the twin strands of Shyamalan's DNA, it seems to me—the very things that will keep him on minds and movie screens for years. A profound sincerity. And a profound ambition. We would never have known the one without the other.

The Director of Fear

David Denby / 2002

From the *New Yorker* (August 12, 2002). Reprinted by permission of David Denby and the *New Yorker* © Condé Nast.

David Denby: Tonight's guest is M. Night Shyamalan, whose films many of you have seen. One of the miseries of going through movies in this period is the disappearance of what we used to call a director's signature. So many of the younger directors seem to come out of television or MTV, and so they don't develop a personal style. Now you couldn't see a single frame of Night's *The Sixth Sense* or *Unbreakable* and confuse them with anybody else's movies. Among other things, Shyamalan has managed to make poetry out of the city of Philadelphia, which some of us might not have thought possible. And the great thing, it seems to me, is that you're doing this not as a little independent filmmaker but in a big-money Hollywood atmosphere, and have managed to come out with your own style almost right at the beginning of your career. I know that when the script of *Sixth Sense* was circulating around and a lot of people liked it, you held out to direct. Is that right? Was the thought that you didn't want anyone else to lay his hands on it?

M. Night Shyamalan: Well, for most people, I suppose, the career began with *The Sixth Sense*, but ...

Denby: There were others.

Shyamalan: There was a lot before that. And it all built up to the moment when I finished this screenplay, and I basically said, "I know how good it is, and I'm not going to let anybody else tell me, and what's going to happen is that I'm going to direct it, and that's all there is to it." And basically we went to all the studios. I started doing something that I still do: I don't tell anybody anything about the project prior to their sitting down and opening the first page—I don't sell it in any way at all. I do that now at kind of a ridiculous level, where Disney bought the new movie, with a price tag on it, without knowing what it was. Originally, though, it was intended to let the artifice come out of the process. So we would call and say, "On September 15th, on Monday morning, we're going to give you his new screenplay, and he's going to direct it, and the minimum bid's a million." That's how *Sixth Sense* went in. And they said, "What's it about?," and the agent said, "I don't know." And that was the truth—they didn't know. And that was basically to say, "No bullshit, please." And if they hear truth in the voice—you know, not like I'm selling myself but I honestly believe in this screenplay. I dare you not to read it. And it was that dare that caused everybody to read it instantly. But that all came about because of the lessons learned from other projects that went before it. I had directed two movies, little movies, before that. The first one made nineteen thousand dollars, the second one made, I think, two hundred and forty thousand dollars. And then the next two made almost a billion.

Denby: It was said of Hitchcock that he saw the movie in his head before he started shooting, and, of course, he would—his original training was as a graphic artist, and he used to draw everything out. You don't draw, but you do work with a storyboard guy. How does that work?

Shyamalan: I work with Brick Mason. He was responsible for the two-hundred-and-forty-thousand-dollar disaster. That's when we first got together.

Denby: Explain how that relationship works.

Shyamalan: Well, it started on *Wide Awake*. I didn't know him, and I guess he was just trying to make some extra cash. This young filmmaker came in to do this movie, with a shot list that I gave him at the time—you know, mid shot, wide shot, scene of two kids—and he just basically drew it up. That's not how we work at all now. Now we sit down and basically make the whole movie—we make the whole thing right then and there, in the room, and it takes us months and months to do it. I'm from Spielberg-land, and he's from something like Iranian-black-and-white-filmmaking-land, and so the two of us together have a nice mixture; we kind of represent the opposite sides of each other.

Denby: So it's essentially planned out shot by shot, cut by cut, before a single foot of film is shot.

Shyamalan: Right. You know, *Unbreakable*, the whole movie, is four hundred cuts. If you watch something like a Michael Bay scene, one five-minute scene would probably have four hundred cuts in it. It's an amazing thing: when we storyboarded *Unbreakable*, we counted up the cuts, because we realized how little we were cutting, and it was around four hundred, and the final film ended up being around four hundred.

Denby: Now, what happens when you get on the set? Do you stick to this plan absolutely, or do you discover new things, or throw out the drawings?

Shyamalan: You know, we come from a very organic place, we come from the characters' feelings. And so when I sit down with a superstar actor or something and we do the scene—and it's basically in the back of your head, the whole scene—and he says, "Where's the camera?," and I say, "It's back there," his instinct will be "What are you talking about?," you know, "Why?" And then I will sit down and explain to him with absolute certainty and clarity why that's there and why it's emotionally correct for his character, and then I'll say to him, "If you have a better idea to convey your sense of loneliness in this scene, I'll do it." And then there'll be a moment of silence, and he'll say, "No, it's cool, let's do it."

Denby: Well, you got two very internalized performances out of Bruce Willis. I guess I knew he could do that from a small movie he made years ago, called *In Country*, from the Bobbie Ann Mason novel. But was he bored with doing things like *Die Hard*? Did he want to calm down a little bit and do something that was more interior?

Shyamalan: I think you catch people at different times, and different actors are different—you can only express who you are, and he was at a perfect place when I met him. He wanted to move on, he had grown up and wanted to do something else, and for me it was nice to have very emotional pieces of dialogue or very dramatic stuff said by an Everyman, a bartender, rather than, let's say, an actor like Jeremy Irons. He could have been the psychologist in *The Sixth Sense*. That would have been more straightforward in some sense, but not as accessible in other senses. I wanted as much of an Everyman as I could get, a rough guy.

Denby: I didn't mean to be putting down his performances in the *Die Hard* movies, by the way, because I think that he does all kinds of comic inflection within that action framework that makes the performances very lively and very engaging. Now, when you're conceiving the screenplay, are you also thinking of specific actors? Was it Bruce all the way, and Sam Jackson all the way, in *Unbreakable*?

Shyamalan: It's become that. I don't know why I do that. On this one that I just finished and sold, called *Signs*, there was a group of three actors that just came to me. One big actor and two others. As it turns out, I got one of those three actors in the movie.

Denby: But if you didn't get the actor you wanted would you have to reconceive the screenplay elements?

Shyamalan: No. I mean, I would if it drastically went the other way. For example, if I did hire Jeremy Irons, I'd probably work really hard to bring in more humor, and some more physicality, because Bruce brings with him physicality, so he doesn't have to do anything and everybody feels like they saw something physical. It's different if you see Bruce sitting down in a chair as opposed to Jeremy sitting down in a chair.

Denby: You've got a handle on things, and you're doing it from—I'm going to mispronounce it—Conshohocken, Pennsylvania.

Shyamalan: Well, my offices are in Conshohocken, right.

Denby: But this is big Hollywood stuff we're talking about, with enormous grosses and large budgets now. Do you want that distance from Los Angeles?

Shyamalan: Well, what I found out early was that the reason that my scripts came out of the pile on the desk is because they had a different flavor to them. They weren't coming from the same gene pool as everyone else, and when I realized that I became aware that I needed to protect it. I was an Indian kid who grew up in a white suburb, and who loved Spielberg, and who went to Catholic school but is really Hindu. Maybe that's a pretty interesting point of view. Not many people have that.

Denby: Let's unpack some of that. Your parents were settled here and then went back to India when you were born? They wanted you to be born there?

Shyamalan: Right. They wanted to have me in India.

Denby: What was the emotional significance of that?

Shyamalan: They're just very proud of being Indian, and they had to give up their citizenship recently because of estate laws and all that junk. That was a very emotional thing for them.

Denby: So you were raised as a Hindu, but you wound up in a Catholic school when you were how old?

Shyamalan: Ten.

Denby: And was that just because the Catholic school was the best school in town, or how did that happen?

Shyamalan: Discipline, I think. It matched the Indian ethic of discipline.

Denby: Do you consider yourself a Hindu or a Catholic or . . .

Shyamalan: I've gotten so much of all these different religions over time that I think the parts that are common to all of them are the things that have stuck with me.

Denby: There's a spiritual element in your movies, a sense that your heroes are suffering heroes, that they have a soul, and that goodness is a very positive force in this world. Is there a religious root to that, or is it just your sense of how the world works?

Shyamalan: Well, it's not been conscious, because until I sit down and write I'm about as far away from spirituality as you can think. You know, I'm a bacon-cheeseburger-eating, basketball-watching guy. Then I sit down and suddenly people are having epiphanies, and God's coming to them—I don't know what that's all about. You'd be a better one to tell us what that's all about.

Denby: I don't know where it's coming from, either. Talk about Philadelphia a little bit. It's a somber city in your movies. It's dark, it rains a lot, there's a kind of blue-gray tonality in *Unbreakable* and a brownish one, I remember, in *Sixth Sense*. Does this represent your child's sense of the city, or is it something that came later?

Shyamalan: Well, it's just a great city for me, because it's a very large city but it feels small, and it has such history. Philadelphia has its history on its sleeve, with the buildings and the little plaque that says that Benjamin Franklin stood here. Spending time there, you start to feel that we had the first hot dog, the first ice cream, the first hospital, the first everything.

Denby: Is it possible that a filmmaking community will grow up around you the way it has in Northern California around Lucas and Coppola?

Shyamalan: I think if there was one more filmmaker in the city it would, because crews could work all the time—basically going from my film to another person's film.

Denby: And now do you hire people from New York?

Shyamalan: Philly, New York, Baltimore. Right now, there's not enough work to live in Philadelphia and just make films. So if there were two or three of us working there I think that a whole community could start.

Denby: When you read about the golden era of the early seventies, one of the things that comes through is that these guys got together a lot—they were all friends, and they hadn't quite made it as big as they became. Do you miss that kind of camaraderie?

Shyamalan: Oh, I miss it a lot. I read all about that stuff, about the seventies, just to pretend that I have that. I call those same guys that they're writing about now, and I talk to them, thinking that I can residually be a part of that group, that I can be the rookie in that group. But it's not like that. I went to dinner last night with Ang Lee, and there's really a sense that we don't know anybody else. Maybe it's because we're both Asian—we go back home and just do our thing.

Denby: You're both very close to your families. And the family theme in his movies and yours is one thing that connects them. The father-son or the surrogate father-son connection is very powerful in both of your two later movies.

Shyamalan: In the new one, too.

Denby: Do you want to go into the autobiographical roots of that? I know you have a powerful father.

Shyamalan: He's a doctor. Everybody in my family is a doctor. As for my relationship with my father, I think the twelve-year-old period was a big time period. I can't not write it. With *Unbreakable*, I just forced my hand not to write the version of the movie in which a ten-year-old boy thinks his dad is Superman, and one kid is right. That was the version of the movie that came so easily. I could write that in, like, a few weeks. Instead, I forced myself to do it from the adult perspective of a man realizing that he might be a real-life Superman.

Denby: Could I extend that into a metaphor for anyone who has unrealized powers and is afraid to exercise them? Because that was one way for me into the movie, of all the things that I might do if I just had a little less fear.

Shyamalan: Right.

Denby: Fear of hurting other people, fear of hurting myself.

Shyamalan: Definitely. What is our potential? And it was also coming from the time right after *Sixth Sense*, when everybody was going kind of crazy saying things about me. I wondered what would happen if all these amazing things were true. And, for that matter, what if they were wrong, and it was only luck.

Denby: You've got one character who is completely invulnerable and another character who is completely vulnerable, and that's the tie between them. Have you ever felt completely vulnerable in the way that the Sam Jackson guy does every day?

Shyamalan: Oh, definitely, definitely. I'm going to go to a sports metaphor now. You know, when I play basketball, there are always two characters that come out in me. One is invincible. There's nothing you can do to stop him. Most often, though, it's that little kid. I'm definitely going to lose, I'm going to get hurt, and all that.

Denby: A lot of people were scared by *The Sixth Sense*, and also by *Unbreakable*. Another part of your signature is a sense of something that's foreboding, something hidden within the atmosphere, something that's going to come out. Do you enjoy the sensation of being scared in movies?

Shyamalan: Freddie Krueger with the blood—that doesn't really scare me. What scares me is something like this: if I had a photo of my wife on my desk, and it was face down, and I put it up and I walked out of the room and I came back and it was face down again. That's scary.

Denby: The reason I asked you about whether you enjoy being scared was that Brian De Palma once told me—I guess it was after he made *Carrie*—that he hated being scared, and therefore he made a few scary movies in order to control that, and to manipulate other people.

Shyamalan: Well, *The Exorcist* is one of my favorite movies, and I have a poster of it in my house.

Denby: Let's talk about children as actors. I talked to Haley Joel Osment on the telephone, and I've never spoken to a more intelligent eleven-year-old kid in my life. It must have been a delight to work with him.

Shyamalan: Yeah. He's probably prodigy intelligent, but that's not really what it is. He's a genius in emotional I.Q. And that's why he's going to be a great actor as long as he wants to be. On *Wide Awake*, I'd have to tell the little kid, if he had to act scared, "Pretend you have to go to the bathroom. How do you act when you have to go to the bathroom?" The face that he makes, that's fear. That's the level of how the directing goes. And sometimes you've got to do that. But with Haley you talk about, "Tell me some time when you were really scared," then he'll talk about it, when his sister did something to him, or whatever. And it's for real. And then, at a certain point, he just really becomes that character.

Denby: He seemed to me so mentally active, though, that I wondered, great an actor as he is, whether acting would be enough for him—whether he wouldn't burst the bonds and want to direct and write and run for president.

Shyamalan: Probably. I think that the moment when, or if, he grows up and he is not cute, and he goes through that awkward stage, and the world says, "We don't want to watch you anymore," he'll be able to deal with that and still have a love for this industry. Or maybe he won't, and he'll reject it.

Denby: Back to fear. I think Freud said, in his essay on the uncanny, that what produced that emotion was the return of something that you had repressed. Now, I don't know if that fits your movies or not, but you could say that ghosts represent our fear of death, and a repressed fear of death. Do you have any sense of any one particular thing that is frightening, that's lurking out there?

Shyamalan: In my childhood, I was definitely scared all the time. My imagination was crazy. They couldn't even leave me alone in the house until I was about fourteen or fifteen.

Denby: You were fearful?

Shyamalan: I was really paranoid about being alone, and all that. It would just be crazy. We came home one day from shopping in a mall, and I was probably ten or twelve—again, this image—and the front door was open. And it was nighttime, and my dad was there—my dad, he's about five-eight, and you could just knock him over like this. So he goes and gets our dog, who wouldn't attack anybody on the planet. He goes to the garage, gets our dog, and goes into the house, and he comes out, and no one was in there. I was just terrified sitting there. He says, "What I was scared about was that there would be some mental patient sitting on the edge of the bed, waiting in there." And that was basically what happened in *The Sixth Sense*. If you're a ten-year-old with those images, you either go loony or you make a movie like *The Sixth Sense*.

Denby: The element here that's most striking is that you keep it real in the movies themselves. You don't have a lot of silly stuff going on. Like those corridors in *The Sixth Sense*, with the mother and son at home, they weren't weird looking in any way, but strange things happened there.

Shyamalan: Well, my hallways didn't have blue lights with fans turning, so I don't make my movies with blue lights and fans turning, you know?

Denby: What does grossing a billion dollars in two movies do to you, as a human being?

Shyamalan: There are two different worlds. In the industry world, for good or bad, I'm at a place where I basically can do anything or ask anything of anybody in any studio and it'll get done, and that will last as long as I don't have *Lucky*

Numbers or *Battleship Earth*. But, you know, that's the way the industry is. It's very superficial. My movies make a ton of money, and that's why I basically call up and suggest an idea and they say it's great.

Denby: That's what I was trying to get at. Don't you have the fear that no one will talk straight to you anymore?

Shyamalan: Well, I think that there's an assumption that I know what I'm talking about. What you really want to have is someone to question you all the time. I need everybody to do that, to say, "Yeah, that can work, but here's the problem with it." But the second part of this success is personal. It's not about the money so much as people feeling you're exceptional at something, and then it becomes that you're exceptional at everything. People ask me if they should divorce their wives. I don't know. I make movies.

Dark Prince

Rachel Abramowitz / 2004

From the *Los Angeles Times* (July 25, 2004). Reprinted by permission of the *Los Angeles Times*.

In a field in rural Pennsylvania, the director M. Night Shyamalan is surveying the remnants of his handiwork, a collection of worn wood and stone houses, forlorn outposts of humanity, reminders of an era of when daily life was hard. The houses intentionally echo the lonely isolation of the paintings of Andrew Wyeth, who lives but twenty minutes from here. In prepping for his new film, *The Village*, Shyamalan spent a long time flying around in a helicopter looking for the perfect field, surrounded by dense woods, that he'd seen in his head.

He'd imagined an expanse "more regimented, more rectangular" than the lolling hills at his feet. "There is no such thing in this area like that," he says with a laugh. "You have to go to the other side of the country. I don't mind letting go of those kinds of details as long as it's exchanged for other details."

He points to the trees that stagger along the perimeter—they're an essential character in *The Village*, the cold, stark lair of malevolent red creatures. "It's nice when my crew, even actors, come in and mess up my very pristine, perfect impression of things. But even when you see the movie, it still comes through a lot—my very stringent aesthetics."

"Pristine," "perfect," "precise," "controlled," these are all words that thirty-three-year-old Shyamalan tends to use repeatedly, mostly in reference to his minimalist aesthetic, and mostly with a slightly self-mocking spin to take off the edge of self-importance. But it's clear he's serious.

Despite the muddy ground, the overcast sky, the director himself is rather pristine in a stark white shirt and jeans. Around his throat and neck is sleek silver and black jewelry—much of it bearing Sanskrit blessings for health and happiness.

In his cameos in his films, the six-foot-tall Shyamalan has an awkward, long-necked geekiness, none of which is apparent today. What might have been presumed as arrogance several years ago has mellowed into the jaunty assurance of a young prince who's assumed his birthright.

Shyamalan's mantle includes *The Sixth Sense* ($673 million worldwide), *Signs* ($408 million worldwide), and the disappointing (for him) *Unbreakable* ("only" $249 million worldwide).

He's Hollywood's poet laureate of dread, the purveyor of his distinctive brand of melancholy-drenched paranoia. He's tapped into the pervasive modern anxiety that something unfathomably bad is just around the corner. Yet his films also offer a respite from the helter-skelter speed of modern living. Shyamalan's world moves slowly, decisively. There are few special effects, no swooping, spinning camera moves, just a series of fluidly turning master shots as he exquisitely controls the climate of fear, systematically raising it degree by degree. Shining through the shroud of foreboding are also glimmers of faith—religion without the treacle—a sentiment that certainly has its following in a God-fearing America. The films also end with his signature surprise epiphany, less a plot twist than a revealing of the underlying premise of the film.

He's one of the last original voices in mainstream Hollywood, a writer-director who's working for the masses and not just the art house elite. Much about Shyamalan is a contradiction. He reportedly earns close to $20 million per picture (along with 20 percent of the back end) and yet he offers to carry this reporter's bag. He's firmly ensconced on the Hollywood A-list but acts like a newly minted suburban dad, preferring to live in the countryside outside of Philadelphia, close to his parents and where he grew up. He rigidly and meticulously orchestrates every frame that bears his name and yet believes almost mystically in intuition, which he describes as a kind of peace that settles over him when he knows he's on the right path. He's tremendously confident and yet fastidious about examining his weaknesses, like a minister constantly searching himself for sin.

"He's a gigantically hard worker and he has an almost religious attitude towards the thing he's trying to achieve," says *The Village* producer Scott Rudin. "It's of tremendous importance to him. He also understands that that's not all there is in life. He's very committed to his family."

The sense of family imbues all his films, and *The Village*, which debuts Friday, plays on the distinct post–September 11 theme of how far a parent would go to protect his family. The story is then refracted through the kaleidoscope of the nineteenth-century novel, much like Emily Brontë's *Wuthering Heights*, which Shyamalan was offered to direct but declined to do this, his own take on the genre.

The film tells the tale, more suspenseful than pungently scary, of a utopian nineteenth-century community, founded by refugees fleeing the violence and evils of the city to live in pastoral isolation. Their serenity is threatened only by the evil creatures ("those whose names we dare not speak") who lurk in the surrounding woods. As the film opens, a romantic triangle is burgeoning and the demon beasts have begun to encroach; it will fall to the town's most vulnerable—the blind girl played by twenty-three-year-old newcomer Bryce Dallas Howard—to sally forth into the forest. The characters in the film speak with an old-fashioned simplicity, a lack of irony, which Shyamalan knows might be jarring to modern ears but which he likes.

He was inspired by the view from his period farmhouse window—of woods, a pond, and geese, a serene spot where, as he says, "nothing bad could happen."

"This is definitely the most personal of the four movies," he says. "The idea of me desperately, desperately trying to hold on to my own innocence. I came at it from protecting my own innocence, the value of simplicity, the value of an ethic, a standard. There's something in the walking out to go get the butter, walking out to get the milk—we've forgotten the lessons in that, the character-building in that. I don't want the decisions that I've made to affect my ability to stay or be innocent. I don't want to be forty years from now and not be able to smile for the right reasons."

By his own admission, Shyamalan is veritably obsessed with purity, though it doesn't simply mean the simple life, the traditional values of love, honor and work. It also refers to the artist uncorrupted by ego concerns, by the lure of success, and adulation, all of which he cheerfully admits is "internally intoxicating." It's also a metaphor for the original voice, that endangered species in an industry increasingly filled with sequels and comic book franchises.

If Shyamalan is something of an idealist, he's also a minister who wants a flock. He likes what he sees as his covenant with the audience and sees his originality as "the only weapon I have" in the marketplace. "That's what they're selling—originality. That will be our strength and our weakness."

Shyamalan will soon transform into a full-fledged brand—the film equivalent of that other master of the supernatural, Stephen King. *The Village*, which costs $72 million (about a third of the cost of *Spider-Man 2*), boasts no certified box-office draws. The studio, which has been suffering through a recent box-office drought, is selling the film primarily on the Shyamalan name. Its ABC wing has already replayed his greatest hits, with Shyamalan acting as emcee much as Walt Disney used to do. *Primetime Live* did a segment on him, and thousands of fans showed up at Regal movie theaters in towns across America for a satellite-feed town meeting with Shyamalan.

Since *Signs*, Shyamalan has become tremendously involved in the marketing of his films, suggesting footage for the trailers and ideas for the campaign. (One bit of marketing he disavows was the Sci Fi Channel's [Syfy] promotion of an "unauthorized biography" of him that was in fact a *Blair Witch*–style hoax.)

"It's a real advantage to be able to identify a film as an M. Night Shyamalan film," says Disney Studios Chairman Richard Cook, whose company has tested the concept with filmgoers. "For him, it's really gutsy to be out there like he is in front of it."

"It definitely puts more pressure on him," says Buena Vista Motion Picture Group president Nina Jacobson.

With a laugh, Shyamalan explains that he called the studio to make his name smaller and to get his actors' names (Oscar winners William Hurt and Adrien Brody and nominee Sigourney Weaver) on the poster, but he was told "this is the one that's working." Still, it's clear that the filmmaker is pleased to be the marquee name. "It's almost taking responsibility. I hated me when I was this little kid in high school that hated when people looked at me. Who wants to be that kid?" he says. "I believe that because of the specificity of the process of my movie, there's an opportunity for people to have a relationship with me. I'm the author. I write them completely. They get made directly from my screenplay. It becomes as much like a book or novel as possible. This is about following in the footsteps of the writer. It's a writer-dominated mentality."

Very Careful, Very Risky

A little while later, Shyamalan is eating crab cakes in a kitschy colonial-style restaurant off the interstate. He's the only face of color surrounded by chunky suburbanites and Andrew Wyeth prints. He's been talking about his film but gets distracted by the waitress and begins to riff as if she's a character who has walked into his film. "She's interesting, with the dyed hair and the smoker's voice. I just love trying to analyze people and where they come from." He guesses about the waitress, "From a girl who's trapped in a town and then rebels who may end up being one of those overweight women in the car who pulls up next to you at a traffic light." He sighs. He pointedly lives away from the media centers, from the worlds where the stars never have to interact with the hoi polloi. "How did that happen? Just the constant numbing of life."

As Shyamalan describes the woman, she somehow seems more alive, as if the deeply internal struggles could rise to the poignancy of art, instead of simply women's magazines and self-help books. His is a writer's gift, and he plays the game with other better-known figures, like the stars of his film. Of William Hurt, he says, "An extremely intelligent man who has unbending ethics and values that the world is continually failing to achieve. You're in the presence of a man who's teaching you." Of Sigourney Weaver, he adds, "She has a majesty about her. She's never going to be dragged down into the mud."

Shyamalan writes his scripts with actors in mind and spends a long time on the conception of the film, jotting down notes in beautiful leather-bound notebooks and then writing draft after draft of the screenplay. Unlike almost any other director working today, he also storyboards for six months, working with a storyboard artist who meticulously draws pictures of every scene in the movie. "It's tedious, and everybody fights you on it from beginning to end," he says. "It's at once a very, very controlling thing to do and at once a complete act of faith."

"That's very intimidating for an actor who thinks he has a contribution to make," Hurt recalls. "I had a moment of anxiety about that, but I realized very soon it wasn't about that at all. It wasn't about restriction. It was about having a structure with a guideline that we could meet or change. He had one criterion: If we came up with an idea, try to be succinct, which is terrific for an actor. To be on the set with Night and Roger Deakins (the cinematographer), it's like being inside a crystal. It's very, very clean and precise but gentle. You know there are ten million details coming together."

"I think one of the surprises for us was that he did every scene—if he could—in one shot," Weaver says. "One of the reasons big movies aren't as much fun is that they have the budget to do masters and three-shots and two-shots and angles and close-ups. Usually it's on the low-budget films you're flying by the seat of your pants. Some of the scenes of the elders [the village leaders, of whom Weaver is one] were [focused] always on our backs even when we thought our reactions were important. Actually, backs are articulate, and it was a daring thing to do and in keeping in the austerity of *The Village*. All the slow pans across people's backs and then looking at one face or two."

Shyamalan shoots no coverage, the customary practice of filming a scene from a multiplicity of angles and reassembling it in the editing room. There are consequently almost no cuts.

"It's very risky," Shyamalan allows, "but risk keeps everyone at the edge of their talent. That's why I hired theater-trained actors, who could go two, three, four minutes and go with that energy flow." He also required the actors to attend three weeks of rehearsal, including a week staying in tents for a kind of boot camp in nineteenth-century practices.

"It was a lot of unself-conscious time together with people who spend a lot of time being watched, and aren't watched for a change," Hurt says. "Studying basket weaving and how to make fires. You have to really commit to making fire with a stick, especially when the matches are right down on the floor and you're freezing your butt off."

"It took us a whole day to make a meal for the group," recalls Weaver, laughing. "The butter was like soup, and the cheese was tasteless. Whatever the French know, we needed some of that."

The director is a great believer in intuition, of just knowing things. Sometimes the instincts seem random. As a kid, he became convinced that a girls school would play a part in his life; it's now where he sends his kids. "Most of my decisions—and it drives my wife crazy—I gut completely. That's it. That's the way to do it."

The director counts casting unknown Bryce Howard as the lead of his film as his latest example of instinct. The director had been talking to Kirsten Dunst about playing the lead in the film, and wrangling over her schedule, and her inability to come early to prepare. Rudin had suggested Howard, the daughter of director Ron Howard, for a smaller part and the director, who doesn't usually go to the theater, came to see her in a New York production of *As You Like It*.

He later called Rudin and told him, "Bryce, she's the one. She should be in the movie," Shyamalan says. "Don't you want to audition her? No. Why? It's not out of anything other than I felt magic and magic is a very, very rare thing to feel. It's a kind of peace about it."

From Basketball to Bond

As a seven-year-old, Shyamalan was obsessed with getting into the *Guinness Book of World Records*. "I was going to bounce a basketball for 1,800 hours," he says. When he got a little older, the desire generalized . . . a little. "I wanted to be great at something. I spent 1,000 hours with the Rubik's Cube." He chortles. "That wasn't going to be it."

Perhaps, he admits, it was just the immigrant mentality. The director, born Manoj Shyamalan, is the son of a pair of Indian doctors who raised him Hindu but sent him to Catholic school. (He considers himself spiritual but not particularly drawn to organized religion.) As a kid, he was tiny, and social, and, as he says, "buoyant." "Very entertaining, and I could entertain myself. My parents were doctors, so they weren't home a lot. I was making up games, shooting movies."

At age ten, he was making James Bond films with a Super-8 camera that he'd plug into a VCR. He went on to make forty-four other homages, including many new chapters of *Friday the 13th*. "They were so awful. They were all copies. It was all kind of trying on the clothes of this person, that person."

Around sixteen, he began thinking about his own identity. That's when he adopted "Night" as his middle name, drawing it from a book about the Lakota he was reading. "I feel very close to American Indian culture," he says now. "It's very much about getting back to the land and simplicity. It's a connection to nature." He begins to riff, pointing out along the way that much of how he feels about the name comes from now, 2004. "In that word is the unknown, lack of information, so there is potential. You're kind of nervous about it but . . . it's just because it's unknown."

Despite coming from a clan of doctors, Shyamalan opted for NYU film school, where he met his wife, Bhavna, and proposed with a fortune cookie. In 1992, he scrapped together $750,000 mostly from family members and shot and starred in his first film, *Praying with Anger*, about an American finding his roots in India. It grossed $7,000. His next film, *Wide Awake*, is a sentimental fable about a Catholic schoolboy searching for God. The film is earnest and dull and earned Shyamalan ritual humiliation at the hands of Miramax cochairman Harvey Weinstein, who according to several accounts recut the film and treated the director brutally.

Years and much success later, Shyamalan blames himself for what happened but finds value in such failure.

"I don't think you can be the best at what you do or be the best person with who you are unless you have that incredibly cathartic, difficult thing that says: 'The world is not going to help you at all. What do you have left?'

"What's left? After everything that's gone, all your desires, all your aspirations, all your pride, everything has been crushed, there's nothing left. What's left? And all that was left was telling stories. I just like telling stories that were not intended for anything.

"It turns out the way I spoke was very accessible to people, but it never would have happened if *Praying with Anger* or *Wide Awake* were moderately successful. There were all these silly, silly things I was considering at the time, of doing writing and directing, and if I had any success at all—any—I would've done the wrong thing.

"In a way, the greatest moment for me is almost failure. Then everything washes away, and all that's left is that thing, intuition, which is there, and says, 'Get up and do this.'"

The rest of the Shyamalan narrative takes on a wonderful Horatio Alger glow. Undaunted, Shyamalan holed up in his home outside of Philadelphia and wrote *The Sixth Sense*. He flew to Los Angeles, checked into the swank Four Seasons hotel, gave it to his agents on a Saturday, and told them to auction it on Monday. The minimum bid was $1 million, and he'd have to be guaranteed to direct. Disney bought the film for $3 million, beginning what has been a multiyear relationship.

It's strange, driving around the back hills of Pennsylvania with Shyamalan: He's much less interested in talking about his startling successes than analyzing his missteps. He returns the topic repeatedly to *Unbreakable* (which he regards as a child that no one loves except himself) and dissects his need for emotional restraint, which sometimes thwarts the audience's desire for emotional closure. For someone who operates from his gut, he operates in a constant state of rigorous self-examination. He seems to be constantly reminding himself to stay, as he says, "pure."

When he sat Hurt, Weaver, Brody, Howard and Joaquin Phoenix down for the first read-through, he didn't want anyone mumbling their way through, as actors are wont to do. "I'm going to assume the movie's a failure," he told them. "I want to look back at this moment at this table and say I sat with the world's best actors."

He exhorted them to make the moment count, and he would do the same. "That's all that we have is this right here," he told them.

Many months later, the director, sounding intensely vulnerable as his film is about to enter the public arena, says again: "If the movie's a failure, I have all of that. It was built on the right thing."

Blue Scare: Shyamalan's Winning Recipes

Gérard Delorme / 2004

From *Première* (August 2004). Reprinted by permission of Gérard Delorme.

Since Hitchcock, we have not seen anything more precise. The director of *The Village* is a goldsmith who thinks about the slightest flaw in his characters, the meaning of each color, the dosage of the smallest sound. On the occasion of his latest film, he explains himself in detail: tips, tricks and instructions . . .

For Shyamalan, chance is good. Every event, good or bad, is a sign of destiny that one must know how to interpret. To support his theory, he likes to tell the story of the setback that determined his professional life: when he was thirteen years old, Manoj (not yet called Night) was waiting at the New York airport for his grandparents from India. The plane was delayed, so Shyamalan went to buy a book to wait. He came across Spike Lee's book about how he made his first film without money or support. This demonstration of faith in himself so impressed the young Shyamalan that he decided to become a filmmaker. Without this twist of fate, he probably would have been a doctor, like his parents. Joseph Conrad's *Heart of Darkness* is another book that made an impression on Shyamalan because it says, in essence, "Angels guide everyone on the only path that is meant for them." For Shyamalan, there is a corollary: if they chose another path, the angels will not be there. So, we have to keep our eyes open. All of Shyamalan's philosophy is contained in this positive, voluntaristic, vaguely New Age approach.

Much has already been said about the career of this prodigy, often described as the new Spielberg: his frenetic appetite for writing and filming, his religious upbringing (Hindu at home, Catholic at school), his first failures, until the shocking revelation of *The Sixth Sense*. Behind his success, there is an exceptional intelligence of cinema, coupled with a colossal power of work. Like a grammarian, Shyamalan thought about the different tools of the cinematographic language, broke them down and, one by one, amplified their possibilities. As a claimed heir to Hitchcock, and unlike filmmakers who edit their films, Shyamalan directs most of his before shooting them. His association with storyboarder Brick

Mason is crucial in this sense. To be convinced of this, it is enough to refer to the chapter devoted to this question in the supplements of the DVD of *Sixth Sense*. From the very beginning of the film's preparation, the director makes decisions as important as where to place the camera or the actors. For example, the storyboard may reveal that in certain circumstances a character in profile will appear indifferent, hence the need to show him or her from three-quarters. Preparation also allows for the preordering of specific sets or props, such as the doorknob needed to portray Haley Joel Osment's reflection.

Until now, circumstances have always allowed Shyamalan to film in or near his hometown of Philadelphia. Probably for the same reasons that John Lasseter and his colleagues at Pixar moved to San Francisco, George A. Romero to Pittsburgh, or Andrew Davis to Chicago. A way to show their independence from Hollywood. As usual, *The Village* is a film that bears the mark of Shyamalan and, as usual too, it stands out from the previous ones and shows the evolution of its author. We asked him to tell us about his process, deliberately leaving out certain questions that would detract from his traditional final revelation. That is why, in spite of an extremely clear speech and under the apparent simplicity, one must know how to read between the lines.

Don't Show Too Much, Too Soon

"At the beginning of a movie like *Alien*, the viewer doesn't know the nature of the threat. The first clues may be limited to repercussions. First, we see a victim. Then the reflection of the threatening entity. Gradually, we get there—to the creature—but by taking its body. And, at the moment of showing it, it is necessary to show it full. At a hundred kilometers an hour. Without hesitation. This combination of restraint and brutal exposure is decisive."

Don't Be Afraid to Talk about the Battle of Good and Evil

"In *The Village*, the theme is love. Its dark side is fear, the wall against which you run into, which tests the positive theme. It is always the same question: what is the world made of? Is it filled with doom and gloom, or are its acts merely moments that make you aware of your fate? Do they annihilate you or do they awaken you? Your interpretation of the evil deeds determines your attitude to reality."

Take Care of the Frame

"I really like symmetry. Framing in the center is an aesthetic bias that helps bring out the tension. When things are perfect, it means you're reaching a climax and something is going to go wrong. If your heroine is in the middle of the door and the door is in the middle of the frame, you expect a creature to pop out and cut her head off. It doesn't matter if she's saying I love you, you expect something horrible to happen. Perfection gives a sense of precariousness.

"More generally, the position of the subject in relation to the camera is crucial: if you are the subject, is it up to you to move or is it up to the camera to move? The character can leave the frame, continue to speak, return. . . . Playing with the edge of the frame is very evocative and useful, but very little used. To film a dialogue, we are satisfied with a shot, reverse shot, two medium shots. It's like speaking with a very limited vocabulary when you have a quantity of words at your disposal."

Reflect

"I love reflections. They are very metaphorical. They are also very mysterious because you can't get a very clear vision of what is represented. Early in *The Village*, we see a creature reflected in the water of a stream. Later, in the same place, we see a reflection of the girl. It's a way of entering and leaving the story in the way of fairy tales. I used them a lot in *Signs*. I also use other tricks like showing things in reverse. It's very disruptive and it can emphasize beautifully what you have to say."

Make Sure the Colors Send the Right Signal

"My daughter always asks me what my favorite color is. I love red, but it's a danger sign. It gets the adrenaline going. If a room is red, you feel more aggressive, it's human nature. Studies show that colors affect emotions. Unlike red, yellow is softer and more euphoric, like a sunny day. Dark and rainy weather makes people sad and grumpy. This kind of opposition brings energy."

Make the Main Character Weakened or Vulnerable

"In the case of Joaquin Phoenix's character, the fact that he speaks badly in public is a handicap. Can someone be a hero if they can't express themselves? I love that kind of flaw. It creates sympathy and allows you to identify with the character. We know very well that our imperfections prevent us from behaving like the heroes we would like to be. This is why it is much easier to identify with someone who is not perfect. Identification is a crucial step in accepting the heroic quality of a character.

"In a western, for example, you will have a hard time liking a character who shoots everyone because he is the best gunman in the world. It's different if, before the shooting, you see him alone, sweating, vomiting and shaking so badly that he can't load his gun. Now you feel for him. You have discovered that he too has a flaw. You tell yourself that you can do what he did.

"In *The Village*, the case of the blind heroine is an example of the beneficial nature of certain trials. In the real world, it often happens that a person who has become famous was very sick as a child. Take George Lucas: when he was a teenager, he had a terrible car accident that almost killed him. I can guarantee you that he would not have become George Lucas if that had not happened. That kind of traumatic incident is what makes the characters so strong. That's why, to those affluent people who do nothing, nothing ever happens to them because they've never experienced that moment of tragedy. It's precisely in misfortune that positive action awakens."

Keep the Family Spirit

"Sometimes your ideas rub off from one project to another. I had already tried to expand the family framework to that of a community in *Signs*. I wanted to give the film a collective perspective rather than an individual one. At the time of writing *Signs*, the family was large: there were aunts and uncles . . . but I got scared and started to reduce them to seven, then five. We were left with the core family. This time I managed to nuance the progression of the collective feeling with the characteristics of each one, taken individually."

Stay in Touch with Your Roots

"*The Village* is clearly inspired by the post-9/11 era, the fear that resulted, the world's desire to be innocent. It was to better emphasize this sense of innocence that I wanted to make a period film. A time when the simple fact of driving the cart in town took two hours. You had to walk to school or to work. Preparing dinner required more effort. But at least you knew who grew the food you were eating. Doesn't this lifestyle make people more likeable? I have a penchant for traditional things. I can't stand to find the TV on everywhere I go. The contemporary world is full of distractions that take away from doing things that are meaningful. Working for others is meaningful. But we've lost that notion."

Keep the Faith

"I didn't want to make *Signs* about religion. I had to find a literal way to show that one of the characters was going to find his faith by becoming a priest again. It wasn't about an orthodox time but an intangible time. It is the same time that is spoken of in *The Village*, as in *Sixth Sense*. A form of spirituality. Here, faith is found in love. This is something that William Hurt says in the film: the world is moved by love and bows down to it with fear. I myself believe that in the world we know, acts motivated by anger will not stand up to acts done in the name of love. It may be naive, but I believe it."

Always Keep in Mind Your Film References

"*King Kong* was a major influence in describing the village. In *King Kong*, you burn to ask the villagers why they need to surround themselves with twelve-meter-high walls. Who do they want to keep out? The answer is a forty-foot gorilla! Here, when you arrive and discover the daily life of this community, you notice rituals intended to preserve it from creatures: women sweep the porch and enter a red flower. You say to yourself, 'Well, this must be a practice that goes back a long way.'

"On the wall of the room, we used to produce the previous films, I used to hang the posters of films that inspired me for the current one. At the time of *Unbreakable*, there were *Crystal Trap* and *The Exorcist*, for *Signs*, *The Birds*, *Night of the Living Dead*, and *Invasion of the Body Snatchers*. We moved and I only have room for two posters in my office: *The Lost Ark* adventurers poster and the Japanese *Sixth Sense* poster. If I had a wall, I would have put up *One Flew over the Cuckoo's Nest*, in honor of the group of actors who played the role in a very serious way while living in a real hospital. It was to seek the same authenticity that I asked the *Village* actors to practice living together in conditions comparable to the nineteenth century. I would also have posted *McCabe & Mrs. Miller* [Altman, 1971] for the description of an isolated village. And a Tim Burton movie, probably *Edward Scissorhands*, because in the last act the movie becomes a fairy tale for adults. My film is not as stylized as those of Tim Burton, but it comes close with its colors and the aspect of 'Little Red Riding Hood.' You could also count *Alien*. It makes for a good mix!"

Prepare Every Detail on the Storyboards

"In the beginning, Brick Manson and I would take six weeks to develop the storyboard. That went up to eight, then ten, and for *The Village* we worked for fourteen weeks, so I don't want it to be a burden, but knowing the flavor of the film at this point is critically important to me.

"Between the storyboard and the result on film, almost nothing has changed. Knowing that the scene is a sentence and that the end of the sentence must end on a specific image, I sometimes improvise by changing the order of the sentence. This happened for example for the shot where the woman finds the first skinned animal. I had planned to start on the treetops, then I would go to the animal before going back to the woman. On the shoot, I saw the camera crew led by Roger Deakins playing with the crane. I thought, what if we try something else, in addition to what is planned? They started on the top and then broke down on the women looking, and it was much better because we didn't know what they were seeing, until the movement ended on the object in question."

Take Care of the Sound

"The work of the sound is what takes the place of special effects for me. It's what I rely on to make the viewer travel like on a roller coaster. The sound effects are definitely the equivalent of the final rewrite of the film. I put a lot of time and effort into it, both for important scenes and for those that seem insignificant. You can change the texture of a dialogue simply by the effects you add on top, underneath, before or after. It's also a way to fulfill the function of music without music. It's an extremely powerful tool, one of the least used in film. It can completely change the course of the story."

Shyamalan's Take

Carrie Rickey / 2006

From the *Philadelphia Inquirer* (July 16, 2006). Reprinted by permission of Even Benn, Director of Special Projects, the *Philadelphia Inquirer,* and Carrie Rickey.

West of Philadelphia, the suburbs shrug their shoulders and the terrain gets hilly and horsey, like a storybook illustration by N. C. Wyeth. In Wyeth country, where artists once lived and CEOs now make their homes, is the weekend retreat of one of America's most successful artist/CEOs. Here, a twenty-minute drive from his "weekday home" in Gladwyne, M. Night Shyamalan comes to a seventy-five-acre farm to daydream and write screenplays at a refectory table facing a bay window that looks out on a shimmering pond.

The willow curtseying at water's edge resembles a nymph descending into her bath. A visitor to this retreat furnished in Shaker chic might wonder if it inspired *Lady in the Water*, the filmmaker's supernatural tale that opens Friday. Shyamalan's seventh feature began as a bedtime story for his two daughters. In it, the phenomenal Paul Giamatti is a super whose faith is tried when he encounters an alien life form (Bryce Dallas Howard) in the swimming pool of his apartment complex. Under her spell, jaded residents join to protect her—but can they?

Losing faith, finding faith, testing faith. The Shyamalan three-act scenario of spiritual renewal connects profoundly with audiences, if not with the critics who slam him as a one-hit wonder whose career has taken a slide since *The Sixth Sense* in 1999.

"That's an easy way to dismiss a body of work," says the thirty-five-year-old with the puppy eyes and dogged work ethic. "That's perception, not reality." Reality is that every movie he makes, if it doesn't gross $700 million, is a perceived disappointment, whatever its merits. If Shyamalan is underappreciated by the critical establishment, he is in excellent company. Says Anne Thompson of the *Hollywood Reporter*, "This is exactly how the critics once regarded Steven Spielberg."

On a sweltering July morning, Shyamalan wears jeans, a lavender shirt and an amulet around his neck. A nimbus of inky hair frames his face. Poised on a couch in his study, where the centerpiece on his coffee table is an electric typewriter of sixties vintage, he resembles a performer waiting to take the stage. The effect is that of Bob Dylan, circa 1967, which is perhaps intentional. For *The Village* and *Lady in the Water* are the filmmaker's protest songs.

The 2004 film, about an isolated religious community, criticizes fundamentalists who shelter their flock from the modern world. The new movie damns cynics who cannot take social action and connect with others in a meaningful way.

In *Lady*, Shyamalan himself plays the second lead, Vic, a writer about whom the lady in the water makes a prophecy. The idea for Vic came from Harriet Beecher Stowe, whose *Uncle Tom's Cabin* influenced President Lincoln to abolish slavery.

"Vic is a link in the chain of events," Shyamalan says. "He's one voice who might inspire another to change the world."

He recognizes this sounds grandiose and makes an adjustment. The filmmaker—who as a child made home movies and as an adult has a foundation that, among its works, fights violence against women in India—explains Vic another way.

"So, when I was fourteen I go to JFK [airport] and wait for my grandparents to arrive from India. At the bookstore I find Spike Lee's *Gotta Have It*," a guide to guerrilla filmmaking. "It never occurred to me before reading it that you could make films for a living.

"So, I go to a film school—NYU, Spike's film school, in fact—and I make movies. And those movies make money, some of which I give to the foundation. So, in a tangible way, Spike Lee is saving women's lives in a village in India."

Here's another story, one unknown to Shyamalan.

Back in '99 Paul Martin, eighteen, saw *The Sixth Sense* in Grand Rapids, Mich. He had been afraid of death, and the movie helped him master that fear. "That's a pretty big deal, I think," says Martin, now webmaster of MNightfans.com. Shyamalan's work influenced him "to look deeper into the movies." He wants to be a director. And that's how Spike Lee inspired Paul Martin to make films.

From the Philadelphia filmmaker's debut feature, *Praying with Anger* (1992), about an Indian American spiritually reawakened by his visit to the motherland, through *Unbreakable* (2000) and *Signs* (2002), his theme has been consistent. So has his box office. His last four films, all made by Disney, have each earned at least a quarter of a billion dollars at theaters worldwide. Collectively, they've taken in more than $1.5 billion. Consider that box office represents on average 16 percent of a film's revenues, and . . . well, you do the math. It's close to $10 bill.

"Only John Lasseter at Pixar can boast a record like Night's," says Thompson. And Lasseter didn't write and direct all his movies. Short-term profits are nice, but long-term resonance matters more to Shyamalan. He uses a different metric.

The filmmaker read in Malcolm Gladwell's *Blink* about the cola wars, in which Pepsi won the supermarket aisle "sip test" but Coke was the victor in the "take-home" contest, being the beverage consumers drank at backyard barbecues.

"I measure the success of a movie by the degree of difficulty plus the aspiration times the take-home effect," he says. Staying power is what counts.

"Using that formula, *Unbreakable* is the best movie I've made—if the lowest-grossing." Though it earned a quarter-billion worldwide, a third of *The Sixth Sense*, it was perceived as a disappointment, "just as *Close Encounters*, which grossed about a third of *Jaws*, was considered a disappointment for Spielberg," Shyamalan notes.

"*Unbreakable* lives on in a Kanye West rap, in doctoral theses, in chatrooms," writes Michael Bamberger in *The Man Who Heard Voices*, about the making of *Lady in the Water*. Bamberger's book, which stands alongside Lillian Ross's *Picture* and Julie Salamon's *The Devil's Candy* as that rare inside look at how Hollywood actually works, details Shyamalan's divorce (or was it graduation?) from Disney.

He made four movies with Nina Jacobson at Disney, parting company after an emotional dinner at Lacroix restaurant in Philadelphia. Her questions about the *Lady* script signaled that she didn't have faith in it or him. Readers of the book might draw another conclusion, that during this disastrous meal it was the filmmaker whose faith was shaken.

"Disney treated me like parents," Shyamalan says. Warner Bros., which made *Lady*, "treated me more like a coach hiring a franchise player."

In movies, as in sports, big talent comes with big ego. All who meet Shyamalan marvel they've never known anyone with such humility and cocksureness. He is thin-skinned and hardheaded. The former makes him sensitive; the latter, impervious to obstacles.

He has something else, too, a quality harder to describe—call it attention surplus syndrome. It's that cocktail of charisma, concentration, and one-to-one connection that Bill Clinton, Oprah Winfrey and Will Smith have.

Are you born with it, or can you train? Shyamalan, who practices karate and plays hoops, is inspired by Tiger Woods and Michael Jordan, "masters at listening to the game," he says. "When Michael got criticized that all he could do was dunk, he mastered the jumper."

And when Shyamalan got criticized that all he could do was make movies with twist endings, he took a different shot. Like *Signs*, *Lady in the Water* doesn't end with an O. Henry surprise. "You lose by doing that, though," he says wistfully, "because you enjoy dunking."

"Night could have gone for easy money, he could have played the game in Hollywood's backyard," says Thompson. Instead he took the high road, balancing the creative with the commercial.

Still, there are industry insiders who can't believe that he passed on writing the *Indiana Jones* sequel, on directing *Life of Pi*, and, if rumors are true, on making the final two installments of *Harry Potter*.

"There was a giant, giant movie my daughters wanted me to take," Shyamalan admits, refusing to say whether said film is *Harry Potter*. "But the studio couldn't promise me control.

"I explained to my daughters that I speak a certain way and that I wouldn't make this movie if I couldn't talk like myself."

His refusal to accept Hollywood's gifts strikes some in that insular community as ungrateful. His belief—that if he has something original to say the audience will come—is a reproach to those executives who bet on sequels and clones.

"Night could become another John Sayles, the artist who walks alone and doesn't listen to any other voice but his own," says Thompson. "Or he could be as respected and successful as Steven Spielberg, who is more of a collaborative artist."

Shyamalan politely allows that his geographical distance from Hollywood "may engender mutual mistrust and suspicion." Yet he can't resist adding, "I've made four studio movies, super-personal, from my original screenplays. Except for the Pixar films, they're the most successful four consecutive originals Hollywood has had in the last decade."

He has an estate in Gladwyne, about 75 acres on the farm, and another 123 acres not far away, plus a loft in New York's Tribeca. His staff includes a chef and a chauffeur. Can Shyamalan stay attuned to the life of ordinary Americans when he doesn't live like them?

"Family is a universal. Faith is a universal," says Shyamalan, a Hindu-born, Catholic-educated filmmaker who increasingly is interested in Buddhism. "And so is being vulnerable and caring for others."

Speaking of which, there's another consistent Shyamalan motif that's prominent in *Lady*. The person who imagines he is healing others invariably turns out to be the one who is healed.

"If you help others, you help yourself," he says. "Are we in too cynical a time that that message is seen as inane?"

M. Night Shyamalan: The Art of the Creepy Movie

Neal Conan / 2006

© 2006 National Public Radio, Inc. Transcript from an NPR news report was originally broadcast on NPR's *Talk of the Nation* on July 20, 2006, and is used with the permission of NPR. Any unauthorized duplication is strictly prohibited.

Neal Conan: This is *Talk of the Nation*. I'm Neal Conan in Washington. In just a few moments, director M. Night Shyamalan joins us. But first, an update on the Middle East.

The fighting continued in Lebanon today. Israeli ground troops crossed the border for a second day in a row to engage Hezbollah guerillas and to investigate positions along the border. Israeli warplanes also launched a number of strikes on Beirut's southern suburbs, the area where Hezbollah has its headquarters. There were also attacks in the eastern part of the country in the Bekaa Valley.

United Nations Secretary General Kofi Annan today called for an immediate end to the fighting. Secretary General Annan said that a quick end would not only allow aid workers to reach those in need, but would give diplomacy some chance to work, though he also conceded that the conditions for a ceasefire did not seem optimal, at least not right now.

The State Department said earlier today that Secretary of State Condoleezza Rice could travel to the region as early as next week. She is headed later today to New York City to meet with Secretary General Kofi Annan and with representatives from the UN mission that was recently in both Lebanon and Israel—that brought what it said were concrete ideas to both sides.

Tomorrow on *Talk of the Nation*, it's SCIENCE FRIDAY. Ira Flatow will be here with an update on what's next for stem cell research. Plus wind power versus the Department of Events.

Today: the new movie *Lady in the Water*. After the phenomenal success of *The Sixth Sense*, writer/director/producer M. Night Shyamalan became—at the age of twenty-nine—the kind of filmmaker who could draw an audience with just his name. His spooky suspense thrillers have generated more than $1.5 billion at the box office, worldwide. His latest film is called *Lady in the Water*.

[*Soundbite of movie*]

Paul Giamatti (As Cleveland Heep): Hey, I saw you. I saw you.

[*Soundbite of bubbles*]

Giamatti: Come out of that pool right now.

Conan: *Lady in the Water* is based on a bedtime story the director wrote for his daughters. The movie stars Paul Giamatti and it opens nationwide tomorrow.

If you have a question about this film or M. Night Shyamalan's others, about the movie business, give us a call, 800-989-8255. That's 800-989-TALK. Email us talk@npr.org.

And M. Night Shyamalan joins us now from the studios of member station WXPN in Philadelphia. And welcome to *Talk of the Nation*.

M. Night Shyamalan: Hey. Thank you for having me.

Conan: And I described you as a writer/director/producer. And I should add, especially for this picture, actor.

Shyamalan: Oh right. Yeah, I mean, you know, it's kind of from the independent roots. I'm kind of doing everything. It's kind of a feeling of always wanting to have the movie feel small, and kind of crafted, and homegrown—even though they're kind of released on thousands of screens. I still want to have that foot in the independent world, East Coast independent world.

Conan: And you cast yourself as a writer. Quite a stretch.

[*Soundbite of laughter*]

Shyamalan: Right. Yeah, the idea of playing this guy, you know, who's a struggling writer, was just very, very poignant to me and very connected. There's something, you know—you write for a reason or you direct a group of actors for an artistic reason. And this particular character, kind of the plight of him—of him not, you know, not realizing that he's writing something that has important consequences is a poignant kind of thing.

Cause we as writers, we don't have a chance for somebody to come in and tell you that, you know, what you're writing is valuable. Or you know, you just sit there in kind of an abyss of insecurity, and it's a poignant struggle. And I think everybody—every time a writer sees another writer in art, they're like, whoa, I feel so much about that guy.

Conan: Hmm. Well, let's listen to a clip of your performance from the movie.

Shyamalan: Okay.

[*Soundbite of movie*]

Shyamalan (As Vick Ran): I know it's a bad time to write. It's actually just my thoughts and all the cultural problems, and thoughts on leaders and stuff. I don't know who you're going to want to publish this thing.

Conan: That was you as Vick Ran, one of the tenants in this apartment building in Philadelphia where this story takes place. Why did you decide, though—you've been in cameos, Hitchcockian cameos in all of your previous films—why'd you give yourself such a much bigger part?

Shyamalan: Well, actually, that's kind of the perception what you just said, and it's not actually the reality. The reality is I've done seven movies. The first one was actually in India and I was kind of the lead in that movie. And it was an independent movie made for nothing. And kind of straight, you know, the straight, independent thing where you write, direct and act. And it's always—all three of those always interest me.

And then in the second movie, *Wide Awake*, I wasn't in it at all. And in the third one, which was *Sixth Sense*, I had a little bit of a part in there, a small part. And then in *Signs*, I had a pretty decent supporting part there with Mel, and it was very rewarding to kind of contribute to the movie in an emotional way.

That's my preference. I don't, you know, the whole cameo thing, like you just said, is the only thing that we have as a kind of—what's the word—clothes that have been worn before. And so the assumption is oh, that's what you're doing, you're doing the Hitchcock thing.

Conan: Right.

Shyamalan: But that's not what I'm doing. And I don't do the Woody Allen thing either. There's just, you know—occasionally, if the part that I'm writing really speaks to me, I'll play it, you know. In *The Village*, there wasn't an appropriate place for me in all those white people, so I chose to bow out of that one. But you know, case-by-case, if it speaks to me, that kind of thing.

I can't do more than a supporting part because I'm not able to do the directing and the writing with the proper focus.

Conan: Let me ask you, though, about the character of the film. That clip we played at the beginning makes it sound like, you know, another spooky thriller—and to some degree it is—but this film is a departure, at least from the four films of yours that we've seen.

Shyamalan: Yes again, you know, it's tricky for me because, you know, I—you know, the things that you asked me are the general belief systems, that I've made four films that are alike. But in reality, you know, *Unbreakable*, you know, I'm not sure how that fits into the group of—if you wanted to say that they're all scary movies—because *Unbreakable* is not really a scary movie.

And for me, *The Village* is kind of a drama. That's kind of covered with this lie, this very dark lie that's going on. And *Lady* for me is, you know, in the vein of kind of like a thriller/fantasy kind of thing. Because I guess I need—the genre for me is that I'm usually doing differently, is fantasy. And *Signs*, it was kind of sci-fi, and then obviously *Unbreakable* it was, you know, comic books, and in *Sixth Sense* it was the horror genre.

And so each of the—again taking a B-genre and then bringing it in to kind of a more modern world is kind of, you know, I like that.

Conan: None of those—you'll forgive me—but none of those were exactly chuckle-fests. This film is funny.

Shyamalan: All right. You know, I enjoyed in *Signs* that the comedy with Joaq, with the tin-foil helmet. You know, there was a lot of written humor in that. And Mel was quite funny running around, cursing, trying to curse, and outside the building, and so . . . And I remember watching it in the screening and feeling like wow, that's a really powerful tool to have alongside the scary stuff as tension, you know, tension relief.

And so in *Lady*, there's a lot—there's definitely a lot of humor in it with Paul, Paul Giamatti, and also. . . . Hopefully the idea was to kind of laugh at it until it becomes poignant.

Conan: Here's an email question from Mike in Winston-Salem. Does it bother you when critics review your films and totally miss the key points you're making?

Shyamalan: Yes, you know, I guess I'm just going to have to come to terms with that because we're going to get slaughtered again tomorrow, when we open. And now it's just a ritual. Every time the movie opens you just get slaughtered, and the movie goes on and everyone forgets that you, that the critics didn't like it.

I mean, I got slaughtered on *Sixth Sense* and nobody remembers that. And nobody remembers any of them, to be honest, actually. And that's the only kind of solace I have, is that—I'm not sure what the deal is with me and critics.

In this particular one, I openly went at them, but I don't know what the deal has been in my career. I, you know, rub them the wrong way for some reason. They're very suspicious of me. I'm not sure what that's all about, but it's hurtful, actually.

I can't say it's not hurtful, because it is hurtful. Every, you know, every opening you just get trashed, and then as the days go by the movie starts to take on its own life. And you know, after a year goes by, everyone thinks of it as an artistic achievement.

Conan: In this film you cast Bob Balaban, the actor, as a film critic. Here's a clip of him giving some advice to Paul Giamatti.

[*Soundbite of movie*]

Bob Balaban (As Harry Farber): There is no originality left in the world, Mr. Heep. That is a sad fact I've come to live with.

Giamatti: Well, if there was a—a mystery. And a guy had to figure out who some people were—like he had to find a symbol guy—someone who can figure out messages—and a guild of people who are going to be important at the end, as a group—how would you figure that out?

Balaban: The symbol person should be simple. Look for any character who was doing something mundane, but required analysis. Someone who was skilled at puzzles. As for the guild? Look for any group of characters that are always seen together, and have seemingly irrelevant and tedious dialogue that seems to regurgitate forever. Is there anything further I can assist you with during my naptime?

Giamatti: No, no Mr. Farber. Thank you.

Conan: And [Bob Balaban] as the film critic Harry Farber, who comes to a bad end. I think I can go that far without giving away the ending of the movie.

Shyamalan: Yes becomes—the movie is kind of like a little bit of like an Agatha Christie whodunit, after, you know ... He has to find, you know, he has to believe in this bedtime story and come ... Yeah, the movie's about storytelling and whether we give reverence back to storytelling or whether we've kind of, we've seen all the stories already. Or whether they've been, you know, whether we don't believe in stories anymore as a metaphoric thing that can teach us something about ourselves and give us, you know, the magic of storytelling back again when were kids or even in older cultures when, you know, you learned about your past, you learned about other cultures through storytelling.

So really the movie is talking about the power of storytelling. And in the movie, Bob Balaban plays a person that is closed, and feels like he knows everything about stories, and that stories can't do the magic things that they used to do anymore. And so, Paul has to come to this realization about how to find the characters in this story, because he comes to believe that he and other people in this building may be actually characters in this real-life story.

Conan: It's interesting. You said you expect to get slaughtered when the reviews come out in the papers tomorrow morning.

Shyamalan: Yes.

Conan: We were talking to our correspondent, our Hollywood correspondent earlier today, Kim Masters, and she said that the buzz in Hollywood is that you're out of your mind, and this is going to be a bomb.

Shyamalan: Oh really?

Conan: Yes.

Shyamalan: Oh, well, I guess that's ...

[*Soundbite of laughter*]

Conan: You're there in Philadelphia where you live and work. She's in Hollywood. But, and they've been wrong before.

Shyamalan: Yes—No, I mean, I'm sure they say that. I mean, I'm not sure what the deal is, why they're so antagonistic to me. I mean, probably because I'm not there, and you know, I guess you're suspicious of people that you don't know. I mean, it's an unusual movie for sure, but it's—we've had audience screenings that have been the best I've ever had.

I mean, the audiences have gone through the roof on this thing, so I don't know what to tell you. I mean, you know certainly—it's been an unusual journey making movies from Philadelphia, I'll tell you that. Because there's been a great deal of disassociation between the perceived reality and the reality of what's happened.

Conan: We're speaking with director M. Night Shyamalan. *Lady in the Water*, his latest, opens nationwide tomorrow, and you're listening to *Talk of the Nation* coming to you from NPR News.

And let's get some listeners on the line. Let's go to John. John's calling from Brooklawn in New Jersey.

John (Caller): Hello Mr. Conan.

Conan: Hi.

John: And Mr. Shyamalan. How are you doing?

Shyamalan: Hey, I'm good.

John: I'm the gentleman who called, Mr. Conan, about I have—I dream of the future and see these visions. But anyway, my question for Mr. Shyamalan is I—your movies seem to have such a deeper meaning than just fantasy or mythology, and do you pull your ideas from biblical and ancient mythology? Do you formulate these ideas?

Shyamalan: I mean probably . . .

John: And one other follow-up, before I go on to get your answer. Have you ever heard of the story the Enuma Elish, which is the Mesopotamian book of human creation?

Shyamalan: No, unfortunately I haven't, but it sounds very interesting.

John: I think if you do a little bit of research on it, it would make a wonderful epic.

Conan: The stories don't tend to be short, though. But anyway, go ahead, John.

Shyamalan: No, you know, the—I think that the ideas are probably based in some kind of religious, you know, thing that I've heard, because I went to school, Catholic school, for ten years. And I'm Hindu by my parents, and I'm actually very, very interested in Buddhism. So I mean between all of those kind of, you know, wonderful stories, metaphoric stories to teach as lessons and, you know, those kind of archetypes probably did affect me a great deal.

John: Yes, I study ancient prophecy and mythology and biblical scripture, and I'll tell you some of these stories that—your movie *Signs*, for instance, was excellent. Because the first time, I just thought it was about alien creatures. The second time when I watched it, I realized what it was really about.

It was about there's patterns in our life, these little signs we should pay attention to, and if we do, we can foresee events to come—small events like maybe you shouldn't go out today because you found two pennies on tails. And it may sound crazy, in essence there's a truth behind it. Sort of like Dr. Michael Barnsley who came up with the theory of fractals and patterns in nature. These same patterns I feel like in human existence.

Shyamalan: Yes, I mean *Signs* is definitely about a kind of belief in kind of a higher order, that there's a meaning behind the things that happen to us. And if we—you know, with faith, you can see that somebody is there watching out for us. And that's, you know at times it can seem very random and hopeless, you know, for all of us, but you know, actually there is someone watching out for us.

Conan: Let's talk with Tom, Tom calling from Huxley in Iowa.

Tom (Caller): Hi. It's an honor to talk to you, Mr. Shyamalan.

Shyamalan: Hi.

Tom: My question for you is, you know, my experience speaking with my friends—it seems like they measure going to your movies by who can figure out the twist the fastest. And it kind of impacted how they saw *The Village*, you know, because they were all, you know, ten minutes in saying, they got it, they got it, and . . .

Shyamalan: Right, right.

Tom: I turn that off, and I enjoy your movies so much more with that turned off. Have you experienced that at all, or . . .

Shyamalan: Yes, I mean, you know like *Lady* doesn't have that. *Lady*'s more like *Signs*, kind of more of a straightforward but multiple small little surprises at the end, as opposed to one big paradigm shift. And you know, I found—I guess, you know, that that chess game is a little—becomes a little suffocating for audience-goers. You know, even though they can't help themselves. There's kind of a chess game that goes on when there's a paradigm shift at the end of a movie, to try to guess it in advance.

And I guess, you know, when I'm writing, I really didn't take those things into account. Like okay, this is the fifth movie or this is the fourth movie, and what they're coming to the table. And it's the same way I wrote *Sixth Sense*. You know, I sit down and write it, but in reality they're not coming to table the same way they came to the table on the *Sixth Sense*.

Tom: Right.

Shyamalan: And I guess that I've become aware of. And so, you know, I guess it gets worrisome for me when I do think of an idea now, with a twist ending. About you know, the chess game that's going to go on in that, you know, if it is a dance—let's say a whole movie is a dance, that that one dance move will dominate so much that it will eradicate all, everything else that you're doing.

Tom: Very good. I'm looking forward to the film tomorrow. Thank you very much.

Shyamalan: Oh cool, man, take care.

Conan: Thanks for the call, Tom. And we just have a little bit left, of time left with you.

Shyamalan: By the way, I just wanted to get back to the whole, kind of the perception versus reality.

Conan: Sure.

Shyamalan: I mean there's a sense of like, you know, like my best-reviewed movie is *Signs*, which people would not realize. You know what I mean? And the reason that that's the one that's the most—I believe it's because it's the most popcorn of the group. And the more that the movies try to be something more meaningful, the critics just have an animosity towards that, that kind of aspiration that it actually it could be meaningful, or art. You know, it's like hey, just stay and do your stupid movies. And it's almost like this unconscious feeling of resentment towards, who do you think you are? You actually think you can do something meaningful? And I just don't respond to that. I respond to kind of dreaming, you know, dreaming positive things for all of us—for myself, for everybody in a hopeful manner. And, you know, I, you know, the screenings of this movie have been unbelievable, unbelievable. We've, you know, it's kind of like there's a feeling that I had when I saw *E.T.* That was a kind of a—I know it was more than just a kid an alien, you know what I mean? You could break it down and say it's only about a kid and an alien and that's why people loved it, but it was religion to me. And the people that actually have seen *Lady in the Water*, we showed it [to] three audiences, just Joe-Schmo audiences, and they've been incredible, incredible, that feeling of like I saw something more than a movie.

[*Soundbite of music*]

Conan: M. Night Shyamalan, who will be turning to the sports section first thing tomorrow morning. Thanks very much for being with us.

Shyamalan: Take care, man.

Conan: M. Night Shyamalan, writer, director of *The Sixth Sense*, *Unbreakable*, *Signs*, and *The Village*. His latest, *Lady in the Water*, opens tomorrow. I'm Neal Conan, NPR News, in Washington.

Persistence of Vision

Leonard Guercio / 2008

From *studentfilmmakers* (June 2008). Reprinted by permission of Leonard Guercio.

The release of *The Happening* from 20th Century Fox marked M. Night Shyamalan's eighth feature film as a writer/director. His rise as a feature filmmaker is nothing short of phenomenal. Since the blockbuster success of *The Sixth Sense*, he has earned an autonomy that very few mainstream Hollywood film directors have been able to achieve. Yet his films read more like those of an independent filmmaker. They are sometimes bizarre, yet always thought-provoking and emotionally engaging. To shed some light on the unique arc of his career, perhaps a personal anecdote is in order.

The first time I met Night was at a party the day before he was to begin production on *Signs*, which starred Mel Gibson and Joaquin Phoenix. Frankly, I was surprised to see him there, and I told him so. Quizzical, he asked why I should be surprised. I told him that if I were in his position, with a feature film starting the next day, I'd be too preoccupied to enjoy myself. He smiled gently and said: "Well, if you're organized, you can make time to enjoy other important aspects of your life—like spending time with friends and family." I was genuinely impressed and understood immediately that a large measure of his success is fundamentally tied to his balanced perspective on life and work. Of course, natural talent, confidence and self-discipline are some of his other proven attributes.

At the time of this interview, he had just signed a prospective three-picture deal to produce and direct the first of the big-budget, live-action versions of the Nickelodeon Channel's anime series *Avatar*. To avoid confusion with the upcoming James Cameron film of the same name, Shyamalan's next film will be entitled *The Last Airbender* and is scheduled for a summer 2010 release. Finally catching up with him, I found him to be genial, warm and accessible. We talked about the making of *The Happening* and discussed other aspects of his filmmaking process.

Leonard Guercio: *The Happening* is billed as a paranoid thriller. How did you come up with the idea for the story?

M. Night Shyamalan: I was on the New Jersey turnpike, believe it or not, on my way home from the mix of my last movie. It was late and I was in that hazy, half-asleep, half-awake zone. I saw this image of the highway with trees on either side when, all of us sudden, an entire plot to a movie erupted. The movie idea just came complete from beginning to end! It doesn't happen to me that often, but I love when it does because it gives you a great confidence. Oftentimes, the process of birthing an idea into a useable form mimics how the process of making the movie will go and, to some extent, how the movie will be received, at least initially. I have to say that this was probably my easiest film so far.

Guercio: Even though this movie idea came easy to you, did you write many drafts of the screenplay?

Shyamalan: Yeah, I did. I didn't think I was going to but I ended up writing thirteen drafts.

Guercio: From your first draft to the thirteenth draft, did the film story change completely or were there elements that remained the same?

Shyamalan: There are two fundamental things that changed. If I were to use comparisons to other movies, it went from an *Independence Day* structure—in terms of a very global event—to a *Jurassic Park* structure where they [the main characters] were trapped in a confined area; they couldn't escape and had to survive. When that shift happened, it made it much more of a nightmare movie for me.

Guercio: How did you come up with the title?

Shyamalan: As the screenplay changed, the story became more of an ambiguous tale with the characters trying to ascertain the veracity of the different theories that are being thrown about. Because the plot was couched in that manner, the title had to have an eerie openness to it.

Guercio: Were there any extraordinary challenges in making this film?

Shyamalan: Well, it was a big location movie. I had one other big location movie before—which was *Unbreakable*. This one was even more so. We literally started in Philadelphia and, as the characters moved out into the country, we went out into the country with them. We ended up in the last act at an old house.

Guercio: Did you hit any snags in production or postproduction?

Shyamalan: As far as my movies go, this was a pretty smooth ride. When I boarded the movie, it had a fluidity to it that was unnerving for me. I thought, gosh it can't be this smooth because there is usually something that upsets me. Then, when we watched the final cut of the movie, it had the same kind of fluidity to it—it just goes. It's ninety minutes long and, from beginning to end, it almost feels like you're watching one scene, one long act.

Guercio: Do you think this is a factor of you getting better with age and experience or that the gods were smiling on you with this one?

Shyamalan: I think that certain ideas are much more difficult than others. Take *Raiders of the Lost Ark* for example—now that's a difficult idea. I don't feel the instincts to know how to make that film. You have to find the right balance of the kitschy-ness, the supernatural, the adventure aspect; you have to be invested in who the villains are. That's more about tapestry and tonality and that's much harder to pull off. *E.T.* on the other hand—to stay with Spielberg's films—would be much easier to execute. This is not to say which is the better film; I'm talking about which is easier to execute. *E.T.* has a simplicity—an inherent movement—to it. You're not dealing with 4,000 extras in a field. It's about a child relating to another kind of child.

Guercio: You obviously have great self-discipline. Do you have a daily regimen or philosophy to manage your lifestyle and work schedule?

Shyamalan: Yes. I try to fill up my waking time with positive uses of my energy. For example, I won't spend three weeks to write only ten pages of a script. If I get blocked in one area, I throw myself into another activity—whether it be developing another screenplay or returning phone calls—whatever needs to be done. I always try to make constructive use of my available time.

Guercio: With each successive film, do you try to push the envelope in your aesthetic or technical approach?

Shyamalan: I do get into those ruts or traps of trying to be more complex, to have one more layer of symbolism, to push the blockbuster envelope and be more arty. I don't want to feel the burden of that all the time so, every now and then, I do one just for fun. *The Happening* is probably a very pleasing balance of a fun-summer-ride and a more meaningful movie. One film where I think I tipped too far on the fun-summer-ride side was *Signs*; it was a hair too much for me.

Guercio: James Newton Howard has written the music scores for all your films since *The Sixth Sense*. However, you often change editors, cinematographers, production designers on your films. Is this related to finding a style that fits the story, their personalities, or availability? Or is it a combination of those kinds of factors?

Shyamalan: I think it's a combination of those things. Each person brings his or her own specialty to the table and some people are more accessible than others. Location is also a big factor. One of the things I always come up against is that I live in Philly. Besides me, the one person who stays on the movie the longest is the editor. From production through postproduction, that's almost eight months! If I lived in LA [Los Angeles], I'd be able to work with anyone over and over. But some of my editors are based in LA and, if I want to work with that pool, I almost have to do one-offs because it's just too long for anyone to be away from family.

Guercio: You've worked with cinematographer Tak Fujimoto, ASC, on three of your films. The director's relationship with a cinematographer is different, isn't it?

Shyamalan: Yes. Choosing a cinematographer is almost exclusively about who is the perfect match for the material. Right now, I'm completely in the throes of selecting the cinematographer for my next movie (*The Last Airbender*). It has to be the right match. Before I really know the material, in choosing a cinematographer I'm committing to a look. Not that cinematographers can't do different looks, but you do get a sense from looking at their body of work where their lean is. It's a very difficult decision.

Guercio: How about casting actors? I read that you wrote *The Happening* with Mark Wahlberg in mind for the lead.

Shyamalan: I write my scripts over a long period and, for me, casting lead actors happens organically. In writing *The Happening*, I asked myself who can do this. Who can do this kind of innocence, humor, and likeability? At one point I thought, this feels like Mark to me. I watched [Martin Scorsese's] *The Departed* a few times. I know Mark as a friend and I always wanted to work with him. This movie is a lot like [Alfred Hitchcock's] *The Birds* and I thought: Imagine Mark Wahlberg in the center of *The Birds*. That would be really cool. So I called him up and said, "Mark, I'm writing this script and it's kind of like *The Birds*. Are you interested?" He said: "I'm in."

Guercio: As a boy, you made short video movies. Was there one defining moment—an epiphany—when you knew you wanted to be a filmmaker?

Shyamalan: Yes, definitely. It was seeing *Raiders of the Lost Ark* when I was twelve. But there were really two epiphanies. The other one happened when I read the book *Spike Lee's Gotta Have It*; I was around fifteen years old. I thought: Wow, you don't need to know anybody [in the movie business]. You can actually make movies, and I knew that this was what I needed to do.

Guercio: So did you plan back then to go to film school?

Shyamalan: At that time, the idea hadn't formed 100 percent in a rational way. It was more in an irrational kid "I can do anything" kind of way. I wrote my first screenplay at fifteen—which as you can imagine was pretty bad. But, at the time, I thought it was perfect—with no rewrites, by the way! It just came out perfect! This is literally what I did—this is what a fifteen-year-old does. I opened up the phonebook, looked up "Motion Picture Producers," saw two names, wrote a letter to them, telling them that I'd written a screenplay and that a lot of people were interested in it (a complete lie), and said that, if you're interested in it, you should move fast. I was devastated when they didn't write back to me.

Guercio: It looks like that kind of persistence served you well, in many ways, later in life. On this subject, I wanted to ask you about your decision to study filmmaking at NYU. Both your parents are medical doctors. Was it difficult convincing them that you wanted to be a filmmaker and not follow in their path?

Shyamalan: There was a kind of quiet tension between us—like some kind of dagger that was going to fall on the family. Like, "Oh God, he's going into film."

Guercio: Do you still get the feeling from them that, one day, maybe you'll wise up, give up this frivolous activity and decide to go into medicine?

Shyamalan: Ha, ha! They're so funny. I think just recently they've let go of all that—finally! When they go into a supermarket and they use their credit card and the cashier asks, "Are you related to . . . ?" Now, with them it's like, "I guess you're doing okay." When I told my mother that the President invited me to the White House, she said: "Well, I hope something good comes from this." I said, "Mom, he's not going to give me a country or assign me an area of the planet! What do you want him to do?"

Guercio: Today, with the new digital tools and the democratization of the media, do you think it's necessary for aspiring filmmakers to go to film school?

Shyamalan: Let's put it this way—it's less important. It really depends on which type of filmmaker you want to be. If you want to be the gathering filmmaker—where you gather all your footage and kind of figure it out in the editing room—then I don't think so. You can come at that world in many different ways, like making music videos, for example. However, if you're going to come at it from designing the movie, executing that design, and then, in the editing room, refining that original design, then yes, I think going to film school is necessary. This [method] is the old way—the classic way—to make movies.

Guercio: I know you're a dedicated film guy, but are you planning to make the transition from film to digital cinema anytime soon?

Shyamalan: I'm going to be the last man standing, as far as shooting film goes. I was persuaded to try a DI [Digital Intermediate] on *The Happening*. I didn't like the look and feel of it; it was too cold. So we tried another and I didn't like that one either. That's when I said: "That's it. We're going back to film."

Guercio: You realize, of course, that a total digital cinema is inevitable in the near future?

Shyamalan: Yeah, I know. I just can't reconcile myself to that fact yet.

Another Happening from Director M. Night Shyamalan

Brad Balfour / 2008

From PopEntertainment.com (June 15, 2008). Reprinted by permission of Brad Balfour.

Like his work or not, director M. Night Shyamalan employs big ideas and challenges himself and his viewers with unusual and dark storylines with the framework to express them. After his incredible success with *The Sixth Sense*, *Unbreakable*, and *Signs*, he was hailed as a youthful wunderkind with a special skill at fashioning supernatural thrillers with a twist. Rightly or wrongly, he was saddled with the idea that his films always had to have a trick ending, a secret to be revealed, and each film needed to be marketed in the same way. But then his last couple of films under-performed spectacularly, and Shyamalan was chastened. So when he landed at Fox with his recent summer film, *The Happening*, he was under scrutiny of the studio.

Although known as a purveyor of big-budgeted genre pictures, Shyamalan was able to make *The Happening* for a relatively modest budget (approximately $30 million) with a cast of quality actors who don't necessarily draw in the tentpole audiences. Yet, despite the pressure to perform, Shyamalan has made one strange film.

One thing this thirty-seven-year-old Indian-born writer/director understands is that by basing his films on the realm of fantasy, science fiction, and the supernatural he draws the mythological aura these genres suggest. Like Stephen King, Shyamalan tells stories filled with ordinary middle-class people thrown into very bizarre, life-threatening situations that test their ability to grasp consensus reality and find solutions.

In this case, planetary vegetation has somehow reacted to our civilization as an ecological threat and developed a suicide-inducing pheromone that gets released near large populations. Almost as if the flora have joined forces to express a warning, certain heavily populated areas of the East Coast are plagued by a lemming-like wave of gruesome deaths, starting with an opening sequence weirdly reminiscent of actual scenes of 9/11 death leaps.

Into this scenario come his key cast members—Mark Wahlberg (Elliot), John Leguizamo (Julian), and Zooey Deschanel (Alma)—who grapple with this frightening and unexplainable situation. Once exposed to these suicides, this trio, and Julian's daughter, try to escape the cities and survive by isolating themselves from society at large.

Shyamalan discussed this and more in a recent session before several journalists.

Brad Balfour: How does this storyline reflect your worldview?

M. Night Shyamalan: You know, all these movies, they're all a little bit like therapy—about something that's bothering me or family things. I'm always working them in, in a journal-like way. But [this film] does represent things that are on my mind [right now]. I think everybody in our generation is starting to worry about these types of things. Certainly in an election year, you think about the future. It's interesting, this slew of end-of-the-world movies. There's an anxiety that's in the air, and it sort of mimics the fifties, the same kinds of anxieties that were about our future. Where are we headed? Are we going in the right direction? Is it too late to change course? [I had that] all in the back of my head. I never thought I was actually all that serious a person. But when I sit down to write, I guess more adult things come out.

Balfour: Born in India, a transplanted South Asian of Hindu descent, your nonwestern experiences seem to have influenced you. Plants having a consciousness is a nonwestern worldview; is that part of the spiritual side to this film?

Shyamalan: Definitely. It's interesting because of the Native American culture—that's all it's about. My middle name, Night, it's an American Indian name. That is what I felt so attached to when I was a kid—from the American Indian culture—the relationship to nature, and worshipping the sky, the earth, and the rocks. As a kid, that relationship felt correct, and it feels correct now as an adult. It's interesting how in all our religions so little is said about how we should feel towards nature. It's an interesting thing to kind of get the hierarchy back in line. We're just one of many living creatures on the planet. I had this conversation [with some of the cast]. They asked, "What were you thinking about?" I said, "Jesus." They said, "What?!"

Balfour: Your main protagonist, a science teacher, is discussing limits of rational thought by the end of the film . . .

Shyamalan: Well, I was reading the Einstein biography when I was writing the screenplay. I don't know if you've read it. It's just fantastic. The new one by Walter Isaacson [*Einstein: His Life and Universe* (2007)] is a beautiful, beautiful book. One of the things I was struck by—and when you read the book you may not even see that it's in there, but I saw it there—was that Einstein was this guy [who first] rejected religion and became atheistic, did his wondrous things in his twenties, and got really into it. Then in the gaps in science he started seeing a hand, you know? In his point of view, the hand of God. A divine kind of "Is there something there?" His life struggle was finding an overall formula, an overall thing that could define the design of things, and a belief that it was there. Then he became very religious. The ultimate man of science became a man of faith. In a way, when I was writing Elliot [played by Mark Wahlberg], it affected Elliot. He's just a high school science teacher. He has plenty of gaps in his knowledge of science. I said, "You're just a regular science teacher. You're not going to be the hero that figures out something. It's not like that. But you see in those gaps . . ." He honors those things in the gap. That's why it felt like Mark was the right casting, because obviously he's a man of faith. Because there are things that we don't know. The lack of need to define it in the closest category is something inspiring when I see that in somebody, whether it's Einstein or Elliot's character or Mark. And so it is a question of science to almost give evidence to something else.

Balfour: You have a math teacher, a science teacher and his psychologist wife playing these roles . . . ?

Shyamalan: The movie's really about the state of where we are now in the world—the paranoia, how we feel toward strangers, to each other, to other countries, to everything in the sense that we don't trust anybody. I was saying that Mrs. Jones is the ultimate version of that character—if she kept on going, she would close off everything and distrust everybody. So we went that way in talking about her. Really, that's the part of me that wants to protect myself, and jokes about it, and tries to undermine it. But it's really a delicate thing for me to go, "It's better to protect myself. Let me protect myself like everybody else is protecting themselves." Which is exactly the opposite of what I tell my kids. I tell them, "Be completely vulnerable. Take every hit you can because that'll allow you to feel all those great things that are going to come—love, joy, creativity—all that stuff. It will always outweigh the amount of hits you're going to get. Although you want to protect yourself from those little hits. Really, the struggle of the movie was her struggle—which is my struggle—which is, "Is this person an appropriate way to be?" Which is the way I am naturally. "Is this an appropriate way to be, or is this the right way to be?" The struggle of whether to question it or not.

John's character is . . . the guy with the numbers. It always comforts me to give numbers: "There's a 34 percent chance that we're going to be okay." Again, in many ways, they're similar, because he sees beauty in math as well. So when he tells that story when they're dying in the jeep . . . he tells that beautiful riddle and says, "If you just double that penny at the end of the month you'll have over $10 million." It's amazing, the properties of math. And he tries one last time to teach this girl in the jeep [who is freaking out], "Isn't math wondrous? Do you want to hear one more story about it?" Again, they each see something kind of bigger in their fields. Whereas Alma's the person deciding whether the world is that way, or if it's really a kind of crappy place. Literally, it was an agenda. I know this sounds silly, but I wanted to put the most likable cast that I could possibly put at the center of the movie. You can get a great actor, but if they come from a dark place, and then if you put them at the center of this dark movie, the movie would just become unbearable. [This cast] all comes from a place—they don't know why they do it, but that's their gift—they come from a place of light, all three of them. And to put those guys, and all the rest of the cast—even Betty Buckley, who chose to play Mrs. Jones—trying to have light . . . And then it just messes up. A whole cast of actors coming from light was right at the center. That's why the movie, even though it's so dark, has such a great light to it. When I wrote the characters, they all had some aspects of me, of things I was struggling with or thinking about. Zooey's character is the person that's scared to be vulnerable. They're all scared to be vulnerable, and use humor to deflect that feeling of "I don't want to risk myself."

Balfour: Is it possible to make a popcorn flick with a serious and important message?

Shyamalan: Yeah, definitely. One of the things that I said to everybody, the cast and crew, "This is a B-movie here. Let's get ourselves straight here. This is just a grade B movie. We're making the best B movie that we can here, that's our job. If the movie has something that sticks with you, great. But we're not going to put that in front of the movie. We're going to have a lot of fun. It's a paranoia movie. We just need to pound away. That's our job." I was really clear about that. So in that way, it was meant to be entertainment. I think one reporter asked, "How come you just don't go make a pure popcorn movie and then go make your art movie? It seems like you want to do [both in one film]." The problem is that both are my instincts, to have one [foot] in each place, which sometimes pisses off one group and sometimes pisses off the other group. My wife says, "Just make one or the other." I wish I could, but as it ends up, I think about all these kinds of spiritual things. And I do love cheeseburgers and I do *Seinfeld* and I do love Coca-Cola and I do love Michael Jordan. It's just me. So if I took one side away—the side that really loves to read about philosophy—and pretend that side didn't exist, it would be a lie. And if I pretended I wasn't jumping up and down watching the Celtics last night, that would be a lie as well. So it's that balancing act. I keep trying to be honest here.

Balfour: To get that mix, this film got an R rating.

Shyamalan: I got an R on two other movies—on *The Sixth Sense* and *The Village*. I got an R initially, for the intensity of certain scenes. We were right on the line, and I could always just pull back and resubmit it so they go, "Oh, that's much better." All I did was take out some sound effects. It's always the impact; the emotion was different than what I actually showed. But this one, with the screenplay I wrote, there was just no way to do it any other way. One of the movies I was thinking about was *Pan's Labyrinth*. I was thinking about it a lot when I made the decision, because I didn't want to make it as an agenda. You want to make an organic decision about what does the material want to do. And when I thought about *Pan's Labyrinth*—which had visceral moments of violence juxtaposed against the softer things that are going on against the canvas—it gave it authority and some teeth. For me, a PG-13 version of *Pan's Labyrinth* wouldn't have had that kind of impact. It wouldn't have stayed with me the way that movie has stayed with me. And so it felt like the right balance of things. It was exciting, and it was disturbingly easy to shoot all those scenes. I had such a fun time.

Balfour: What are your greatest fears in real life?

Shyamalan: I've changed my thinking, and my analysis of fear has come down to the factor of being alone. It's all based on versions of that. Take random things that you're scared of . . . "I'm scared to fly" or you're scared of the new job that you have. It's all related to the feeling of "I'm going to have emotions, and no one else will have those emotions. I'll be alone in some manner." So if you're scared of flying but if you talk to the pilot or talk to somebody else, you don't feel as scared. It's the human connection. You're not alone anymore, you have commonality. And I've said that art, I believe, is the ability to convey that we're not alone. That's the power of art. It's always been in our genetics, since we were cave people. Fear protects us—"Don't go down that road, you'll be alone. We don't know what's down that road. You'll be alone. Being alone is not good. Together we're safer." And the person that didn't have that [reaction], didn't survive, right? Now it's flipped on us and become a limiting factor. We're scared to put our kids in the backyard now because our neighbors might do something. But our neighbors are wonderful people; the assumption is wrong. It's the same that it was when I was a kid running around on a bike. We're so much more scared now, but nothing has changed. Nothing has changed, except for fear. And the fear builds on itself, because we get more and more isolated like Mrs. Jones, until your fear has been realized—you're all alone.

The Last Airbender: Roundtable Discussion with M. Night Shyamalan

Cloneweb.net / 2010

From Cloneweb.net (March 2010). Reprinted by permission of Marc Loos.

Question: How did you come to the franchise?

M. Night Shyamalan: Actually, I just told this story this morning at the Nickelodeon convention, and I said this on stage. There was a period of time where I was really interested in doing a real long-form story for the movies. I've been waiting and talking to a lot of people. I had a lot of conversations about *Harry Potter*, every single one of them, and *The Chronicles of Narnia* was offered to me from the estate. All of these different franchises, and I would really kinda think about them seriously. Much to my kids' regret, I would eventually say at the breakfast table, "I'm not doing it," and they would just get upset. "Why? I can't believe you're not doing it. You're crazy!" My wife would just stop listening to the conversations because she thought I was never going to do something that I didn't create. "Why do you even have these conversations? You're just wasting all of our time and energy." So that went on and on; that was like the running joke forever. I was saying this morning that my dad would always ride me about it 'cause then the movie would open and make so much money. [*Comical Indian accent*] "Why didn't you do it?" [*the room laughs*] and I'm like "Dad . . . enough already. I'm happy—everything's good." "But you woulda made so much money!" "It's all good, it's all good. There will be something someday." My oldest daughter is really philosophical and she's like, "Well you're saying no for a reason. There's something down the line that's meant for you."

So while this is all going on, my youngest child is watching a show on Nickelodeon, and she's totally into it—totally into it. And in classic parenting style, I did not pay any attention to what she is watching. One day my mom came over to baby-sit—I remember this moment specifically 'cause it was in the house we lived in before. She was baby-sitting, we were going out to dinner, and she started watching this show that she (the daughter) is obsessed with, with her. My mom calls me from the family room and is like, [*in another comical Indian voice*] this has Hindu philosophies in it! And I'm all like, "Great, Mom . . . thanks. We'll be back, we'll be back." We take off and there's this movement going on in the house and I'm not really paying attention to it still. And then there's the request for a Katara costume for Halloween, and I'm like "Who's Katara? What is this?" I remember in my office we were looking it up; I type in "Katara" and see it's a cartoon, and then still paying no attention to it in the big scheme of things.

Meanwhile, there's the plotline of me having conversations about these other franchises and it not working out while this other little thing is happening—ya know, if this is how I would structure it. Then we went out to go get some books, and this store they were selling DVDs and books. The first season of this show was there, and my daughter was like, "Can we get it? Can we get it?!" and I'm like, "Okay, we'll get it, we'll get it." We didn't have anything to do that afternoon, it was a Sunday—so we all went down in the theater. At the time we only had the four of us, but now we have another child. So the four of us went down into the movie theater and watched the first episode, and we were like, "This is cool, this is cool. All right we'll watch another one . . ." and we put another one on . . . and another one, and another one. And literally the whole day went by. It went from daylight to darkness while we were in there, and we go, "My god, we gotta feed these children! We gotta eat!"

When I was thinking about it, I was thinking it was so weird because it has everything that I love. I study martial arts; I've been studying Kempo for a decade. Obviously I study spirituality of all kinds. I was in a Hindu family, but I am hugely Buddhist in influence. So everything was there. I have to go visit monasteries in France, the whole thing, I'm totally into it! There's that, and then martial arts movie background. Everything about it was just so interesting to me. I've never done a CGI movie because my storytelling is so much about humanity. I love the dinner table scene, but everybody else gets scared of the dinner table scene in a movie cause the movie will stop—I love it! Like *Signs*, it's all built around the dinner table scene: their last supper together. I love it. If it's in a room, I got it. It's the end of the world? We'll just see it on the TV. The whole technical part of it got in the way of how I can think really cleanly and clearly, and tell my voice. Well, in this, when we were watching I thought it was really cool because what they're doing with the elements is related to their emotions and philosophy. And as you can tell from the movies I've made recently, I'm very into nature vs. man kind of questions. So the idea of the struggle with the balance between nature, and the connective-ness to nature was really cool.

So, we leave the theater and go up to get some food. Everybody's over in the kitchen and I open the fridge up and just stop and I was like: "This would make a great movie!" and the whole house erupted. I was serious. My wife, who basically if I said I retire today would be the happiest in the world, was like, "You have to make this! This is it! This is the movie you've been waiting to make. This is you, this is so you." "Calm down, take it easy!" Everybody was just like hyped. The kids were so worried I was going to say no. But I was like, "I'm gonna find out who owns this and find out what's going on." And my wife was like, "You gotta call right now!" "It's Sunday night! I'm sure it can wait 'til tomorrow morning." So I slept on it and brought it to the office. I said how this is really cool, and I think I could see me in this. So I called up Paramount and chairman Brad Grey and asked him to come to New York. I was very cryptic about the whole thing. "What is it about? You wanna make a movie?!" "Yeah, let's just talk." So he came and I said, "Look, you have on the Nickelodeon station this show that I think is *Star Wars*. I would love to make this movie for you." He went and checked it out, and we had another meeting in LA and he was like: "Go make it!"

Question: Can you talk a little bit about the bending and how it's coming along?

Shyamalan: It's about two and half years of research and development on it. We would look at anything that's ever been photographed, even on a motion picture camera, of where I thought the feeling felt good. For me, I've never seen fire that's looked good—I just don't buy it, it looks like it's coming out of a blowtorch. It's very tricky stuff. I have photographed fire, and it looks CGI. It's just very difficult to photograph and make it look real. Whatever it is, the capabilities of film or video, it can't capture that level of difference in light. It just looks fake to you; it looks like it's on the picture. You go, "Wow, this looks really cheesy and fake," and I go, "No, that's literally fire—there's nothing else there." So it's a very tricky thing.

I thought out of all of the elements air would be the most difficult, but we came to the realization that air has no inherent qualities—it's just whatever environment you're in. If you're in a snow environment, it starts moving snow. If you're in a dirt environment, it starts movie dirt. You just have to keep it translucent enough so you know that it's not another element, but the element of air. So there was a careful analysis of each element, and ILM would start to do tests for me and show me different things. Water I really felt like I wanted it to be like when I saw stuff from astronauts when they'd open up a Gatorade bottle and it stays connected, but it's kind of moving. And they touch it and it starts moving again. That was the basis of water; I wanted the water to look it was in zero-G. So they went under those kind of principles. ILM has a huge amount of experience with water in particular. I really like some of the stuff they did with the third *Pirates* and the whirlwind of water as the boats are going down. They have a huge amount of experience. They were the first ones that started this stuff with *The Perfect*

Storm. So it was a real long process, but super, super exciting. Each and every time it had to be a combination of what the character was doing and at any time, nothing could look the same. It wasn't like you could do waterbending twice and make it look the same. And that was the thing, I think, when the burden of what went to such a high level. They would come up with one way effectively, and I was like "Great, now come up with eighty more!"—because nobody does it the same way. That was the fun thing for me because I got to express character through CGI. Then I could really talk to the animators and say, "Katara isn't skilled yet, so it should be very fragmentary with things falling off the edges." I could talk in character like that. Or "This person is angry" and so on.

Then talking about physics, ya know, I just don't believe moving from A to B can be that fast, and all of those wonderful conversations that we've had for two years now. My big fear was that whatever was in my head would look, at the end of the day, cheesy. That after I guided all of these amazing people for two years, we'd look at it and go [*makes an "uh-oh" face*]. Luckily that hasn't been the case. I've been so excited about what we've seen. I love going to watch the new footage every day. I think in the movie there is—if you count every little thing like: they have to put a background in the corner frame because there is a little bit of set you see—I think there are four hundred CGI shots. Which, for a movie of this scale, is very, very little. To give you an example of another film, *Temple of Doom* would have two thousand. That's also because I have very long shots. So with the Pakku shot, you just stay with the Pakku shot. And of course ILM just hates that because you're just staring at the CGI for so long. "You should be cutting for distraction"—"Not on this one, you're just going to have to make it look real good."

Question: If I had to guess, one of the most difficult parts for you to fit into the movie would be the comedy. Was that a challenge for you?

Shyamalan: I think it's the single thing that I am struggling with in the movie, partly because the show is so schizophrenic—in the best way. And it developed a tone as it went on in the series. The opening scene of the movie is the youngest episode of the entire sixty-one episodes—it's so young. Mike and Bryan started out making the show and went for a particular tone thinking it's Nickelodeon, and going a little bit against their instincts and going young. And as the show went on, they just started being more and more themselves, and it got older, older and older—and it became cooler and edgier. But in the beginning he had lines like "You wanna go penguin sledding?!" and stuff like that. That was an appropriate line in one, but would not be in Episode 27. That, which is kind of its origins as it was finding itself, is the balancing act of the movie. I want it to honor that part of it. It would be like taking away why we are all here—'cause my seven-year-old connected with it. I don't want to take that away. I have a very dark and edgy sensibility, but I am trying to balance the two. But the humor is definitely the trickiest part of the piece.

Even on Nickelodeon, and even on that show, the comedy is broad at times. And then you have episodes like "The Blue Spirit" episode, I think it's thirteen from the first season, which is all edgy. Straight up, I literally picked Episode 13 and put it in the movie. I just literally picked it up and put it in the movie. But from the first season and first episode, you're just picking and choosing really delicately how to maintain it. I've actually written a second draft of the second movie, and it's so much older. It's so much edgier and older. That's what they were naturally having to do because the kids are twelve to fourteen at the beginning and they just keep on growing and getting more mature. It just naturally moves that way. Then you have all of these cool ladies fighting, the Kyoshi Warriors vs. Azula's crew, in the second movie. It just gets darker and edgier in the greatest way—more Shakespearean, for me, as the season progresses. So . . . I like goofy humor, so I have a higher tolerance than most. [*Laughs*]

Question: I have the most important questions of this day . . . Is Momo in the movie, and will it be fun?

Shyamalan: Why don't I answer the second one? I hope so! There was a moment when I had my focus group—with my kids—at home when I was developing it, and I was asking Mike and Bryan, "So what does Momo do exactly? What does he represent?" and they were like "Well he's just kinda fun. We would finish an episode and just sorta put him in somewhere." When I was first developing the movie I needed to have a reason for everything. Maybe I was over-thinking it, but I asked the kids: "What would you think if Momo wasn't in the movie?"—they literally attacked me. They were not speaking to me, so I was like, "Oh okay, all right, all right. Relax . . . he's gonna be in the movie." So he's in there. I love him! He seems so real. I would believe that he existed somewhere in the world, so it's a fun thing to have. I think he's just really fun and cool in the movie. I would love to kind of have a moment for him, somewhere in the three movies, where I give him a purpose. That's my dream: give Momo a purpose.

Question: You've filmed with huge stars like Bruce Willis, Mel Gibson, Samuel L. Jackson. And now you have a young but talented cast. Dev Patel is maybe the biggest name. Do you have any concerns at the box office?

Shyamalan: You know, I don't, because the subject is the star. In a way, having the transparency of being able to look past the [actors], and see the story is the best version of this kind of movie. I had a conversation with Paramount where I was like: "Let's not show these kids at all until opening day so that everybody thinks that they're the real characters." And they were like: "Well, everybody knows Dev." "Okay, well nobody see anyone else!" So in their minds they think they're these characters. So no, that hadn't worried me because you have opposite issues as well once you have stars in parts. It starts to just tip in way. You want to suspend disbelief in a movie like this and go, "I lived in that world, and I've only lived in the world for two hours and I can't wait to go back."

Question: A lot of people look at the trailer as, say, "Well, it looks like the entire first series, but it can't possibly be because there wouldn't be enough time for it." A lot of people are curious because there are a lot of really fun, smaller moments like King Bumi and stuff like that. What had to go?

Shyamalan: For the first outline I made for the movie, I brought Mike and Bryan to the house and asked them, "Whaddya think?" and they were like, "This is like ten hours long, you have to cut something." I was like, "I can't! I love everything." Literally, the first outline was so long. I'll give you an example. The bounty hunter with the shirshu, I love that! But I just couldn't fit her in. In an episodic series, that nature is: it's episodic. A beginning, middle, and end in each episode, so it needs you to go right, left, right, left like that. But there is a through-line that is present in most episodes, like how he has to master all of the elements and that kind of thing. Katara and her brother are becoming a family and they're protecting Aang. And they're moving to the Northern Water Tribe. So there would be broad things that represent the story of the first season, but there's bunch of things had to get jettisoned for this movie. My hope is she'll end up somewhere in one of these movies.

I moved some things around, like "The Deserter" (I love him!)—I moved him to the third movie when Aang's going to learn fire. So those kinds of things. King Bumi's not in the first movie, but my hope as we get to earth, all of those earth kind of related things will come in handy. It's really a distillation of just getting the story correct—and how much lay in? I have a line, which I hope stays after the three months, that is Grandma saying something about her friend Hama, which is like my favorite episode in the series—the bloodbender episode from the third season. I wanted to lay the groundwork for that. So as much as I can, do the balancing act. It's always sad to lose something that was fun and exciting in the first season.

Question: What do you think people will be surprised that you kept?
Shyamalan: Let's see . . .
[*Jordan from UGO suggests the Cabbage Saleman.*]
Shyamalan: Yeah, ya know, I didn't keep him.
[*The room "awwwwwws" with slight disappointment.*]
Shyamalan: All of that kind of broad comedy stuff, the movie can only handle a certain amount for you to believe the stakes of the movie. So what I've even found, I had a certain amount of broad comedy in it and if the characters aren't honoring the milieu of what the movies supposed to be—it's a time of war and we've been out of balance—it starts to fall apart a little bit. You can have humor

but it has to be situation appropriate humor. Where in an episodic scene, you can really go broad and come right back and it's not such a big deal. Those kinds of things have been the most challenging thing about the process. I think it's primarily the first season's thing because they were finding the balance as well. In the genetics of the movie, I am finding the balance as well. What is the balance between what is, let's call it "the edgier, *Lord of the Rings*" part of it, and all of this stuff (i.e., the cabbage guy). "Not my cabbages!" and all this stuff. The second season, for me, just laid right out. There's much less struggle. Even the first draft of the screenplay laid right out. You go, "I get it—this is the Shakespearean background and all this stuff." I still have stuff that I shot that I am struggling to hold on to 'til the last second, so we'll see what ends up in the final movie.

Question: As someone who has typically created your own stories, was it difficult to write this even though you were a big fan of the series? What was that like?

Shyamalan: Liberating. The problem with being auteur-ish is you struggle so much to hold on to your vision. That's a great thing and it's a bad thing. You can't see it from a perspective, and be able to judge it honestly. Maybe I wouldn't be able to have a conversation about the tonality because I'm so "it has to be this way." I love the show and I love almost everything in the series, so I know why I would put it in, but I have the perspective to say, "Okay, by pulling out one line here it becomes more meaningful." So I think it's been a good thing. I really enjoy working on the movie, which is the main thing. I think you'll feel that. It's not work to me, analyzing it and getting the balance right. That's the other thing, the Miyazaki influence of the show. Do you guys know who Miyazaki is? He's like my god. He's Michael Jordan to me. I met him last year, and luckily for me he hasn't seen any of my movies. We had a translator. He had his apron on, and he was still finishing *Ponyo*. He was still animating and came back down, and I was like "man, this is the greatest." Mike and Bryan were so influenced by Miyazaki and I'm so influenced by Miyazaki—that's just an honor. Trying to reach that sort of tonality to an American audience. That water doesn't just mean water, it has meaning and something behind it. It's metaphorical. I think in different cultures it is easier to accept that.

When my movies go around the world, like in Spain, right away they'll just take it and anywhere I want to go with spirituality and that stuff. The same with Japan. And then other countries and other places, it's much more: "I'm not getting this. What is this?" United States and UK fall into a brother/sister category in that reaction. I know when I come up with an idea that's more spiritually oriented that these are the territories I have to be more aware of. *The Last Airbender* is a spiritual movie. There's no way around it. I mean, it's badass—it's really cool, but it's so meaningful in so many ways. Making sure that comes through is something that really motivates me. So there's a lot of things that really excite me and make me want to be like the guardian angel of the movie. I feel very protective of it. There's a great connective tissue. The way I feel as a parent to my other movies, I feel that way as well with this movie.

Question: Do you think the experience opens you up to directing other people's scripts in the future?

Shyamalan: Yeah, my family would not back me on this statement, but I am open to that. I am always writing. I'm writing a new movie now. I'm writing a thriller for me to do and I just have a bunch of ideas. What often happens is I'll get offered a movie, but I get offered a movie that needs a lot of work. They'll say come in and rewrite the whole thing and then go direct it. And I'm like, if I'm gonna do all that, I'll just do this one that's in my head. I'm waiting for like it happened with *Airbender*, and it'll happen again. I almost did *Life of Pi*, and that was more timing than anything. I really loved that book, and I thought I could really do a good job with it. So, I almost did that. If I had been offered *Jurassic Park*, I would've done that, but that went to that other guy. [*Laughs*] Nothing would please me more [than] for someone to go: "Here's a source material; a book that you're going to connect with in way that's going to say 'don't do the next movie of yours.'" Basically that's what you're saying. "Don't do the movie you have in your head, spend the next two years on this movie." And that can definitely happen. I've fallen in love with so many books, and I've fallen in love with a TV show—unexpectedly. The more wishful thing is that they hand me a screenplay that is like "oh man, that's unbelievable," go make that. And I'll be like, "Damn, I can go make this movie in like a few months? This is fantastic!"

Question: You talked on the larger scale about how you're envisioning *The Last Airbender* with multiple movies and all of that. How far ahead are you in scripting and planning out this entire story? Is [it] affecting the filmmaking process having an approach with sequels in mind?

Shyamalan: I think "sequel" is a misnomer for this, and I kept telling the studio that. "Is there any way we can talk about this in 'not sequel' terms?" Because it's not like "we like these characters, so let's go on another adventure." It isn't like that. This is a story that has a beginning, middle, and end—and I'm telling you the beginning. *Lord of the Rings* did that so beautifully. But you know when they just made up another story just because. You can tell that. This isn't that. Of course George Lucas did that as well. He had the whole story, and now I'm gonna tell you the next one, and the next one. It's one of three parts. Hopefully they'll like the first part enough that I will be able to make the other two parts. But sequel has, in a sense, a revisiting in a way that isn't that. I completely got into this to do a long-form movie. The first thing we did when I met Mike and Bryan, and I came on—they hadn't finished season three. The first conversation was in my hotel room. "Dudes, I gotta know this. This is critical! This has to end. This has to end. If it doesn't end, I'm not on board. But if you don't want to end it—it's all good." They were like "no, we saw it as three seasons for each element that he has to learn." And I said "great." At that time they hadn't even decided where things were going to end, even like who Katara was going to end up with. All of that stuff hadn't been figured out yet. We had such amazing conversations in that room, but we all agreed, shook hands and said, "It's over. We're gonna finish the tale." I said that I could definitely get behind that.

The last thing that as the contract was closing with Paramount, I just said, "Three. Right? Three." That way I can put a lot of integrity into it and know how to press the accelerator on a storyline or not. And as I am developing it, if I go, "Okay, this is not fitting into the movie," I know how to handle it. Like already I pulled out a couple of things from the first movie that I thought were going to be in the first movie. Now it's going to affect the draft of the second movie. I need to redo the introductory scene of a character because I pulled her from this one—that kind of thing. It's really important for me to have that. For me, the second season was like spot. I just got that season; I felt it. Of the twenty episodes, so many spoke to me. And the storyline was really clear and very exciting. The whole trauma of the way it ends—the darkness of that—I love it! Love it, love it, love it. The third movie (and I can't even think about it right now without getting really upset) I have to really go through and analyze it really carefully. That was, again, very schizophrenic for me. I've got to find it, and I suspect when I look at those twenty-one episodes, I will see that there are the eight episodes that have the through line right there. And then there are all kinds of things—[*he directs at me*] like remember "The Beach" episode?—that have really nice colors, and we'll see what we can do . . . I don't even know if I answered your question.

Question: Have you scripted through? Do you have a rough draft for them?

Shyamalan: I have an idea of what I want to do with three. The only thing I would do differently (and I don't even know if I should say—it's so many years away!) but I was toying with it: I want to know what happened to Zuko's mom. That would be something that I might include. Something you can only come see in my movies. When it finished, I called Mike and was like, "Are you crazy!?! Tell me what happened to his mom!" [*Everyone laughs*]

Question: You're definitely the one that's going to direct all three of these films? You're not going to farm them out?

Shyamalan: I mean, they could fire me! [*Laughs*] Yes. If it's successful on the Fourth of July weekend, and there is enough feeling and momentum with the audience wanting to see the other two, the idea for me is to go direct my thriller in between while we prep for movie two. It just takes so long to prep these movies with the design process and the location scouting. You know how when you watch the *Raiders* series (which is my favorite movie of all time) it went from being very location oriented to more on-stage as the movies progress? I want to do the reverse. I want to get more location-oriented and more reality based as the three movies go. That requires a lot of location scouting. "Can we shoot in Morocco? Can we shoot over here? How can we get a road there? If I want to build this there, how can we get there?" That takes forever to figure out. And then of course the R&D process for with ILM again. Now we're way ahead, obviously, than we were when we were starting from scratch on the first movie. That should be really exciting. I have a great team together now, so that's also really set.

Question: But you wouldn't be concerned with the cast members getting older? Would you ever consider sitting back and being producer and farming out to a directing team a la *Star Wars*?

Shyamalan: I suppose it's possible. You can never say no, but right now I'd say "no way!" Another thing is, my dream is for the last movie, Noah is ripped! He looks badass, you know? He's growing up on film for three years and you're like "oh my god" by the end. He was like a Texas champion already, and I have him training in the off-season. I call him and ask, "Are you training, dude? Are you training?!" He's learning all kinds of martial arts. We want him to be for real—for real.

Question: So. Sky Bison aerodynamics. In animation, you can kinda get away with a big fluffy tail powering a giant beast with three young adults on top. In live-action film, even with geniuses like at ILM, you kinda have to work out a situation. How is this gonna work 'cause we haven't seen any of Appa yet. Obviously this is the big reveal, so can you give us a little insight into this?

Shyamalan: The thing is with Momo and every other creature—the Komodo rhinos and that stuff—it's literally a fusion of two creatures and the physicality is very plausible and dynamic. The way I make movies and the way I was talking to ILM is very specific. You have to believe the physicality and the weight on the Komodo—that it can claw on the ice and go up the wall. And this one . . . you know, my kids sleep with a plush Appa. Literally, I was just like we're going to have to take the leap of faith on this one. ILM and I were like, he's an airbender—we're going to have to go with he's an airbender.

It was funny 'cause Mike and Bryan when they were asked to come up with a show, the first drawing they had was someone in the clouds with a staff and some bisons in the air. That was the very first image. Like there was a shepherd, and his flock was in the air. "I guess he's kinda related to air" and they started working that way. "Maybe there's a water" and that kind of thing. That image though, the Appa image, is the literal beginning of this entire thing. So when we were making the movie, I was like, "We're just gonna go with that. I'm not gonna change it into something that could actually physically fly with wings and all that stuff." Not while the kids are sleeping with a plush Appa.

You know what the funny thing is? He's my favorite in the movie. He's my favorite. I literally can't wait to see him again every time he comes on screen. And there's this one scene where he shows up behind the villagers that are getting attacked and he roars! So you know, it works. Sometimes you just accept the material and you take that leap of faith.

Question: Are you planning on including the "lost Appa" storyline in the second film?

Shyamalan: He's a huge character in the second movie. There was a version of the draft without it. I remember I was in my house and I was like, "Lemme try it without so much of this being trying to get Appa back," and when I tried that I was like, "I don't like this movie. Put him back! This is about trying to get Appa back." He gets distracted from his training because he needs to go get Appa, and it's so compelling because you love him soo much. In the second season and the second movie, it's so much about his character. Having this incredible friend and brother that gets taken away from you, and you're like, "I don't care about this quest anymore or about training, I need to get him back." So he's huge in the second movie.

Question: Beyond the references to the Hindu fire god Agni, and the reincarnation of the Avatar; what other Hindu and Buddhist references are there in the film?

Shyamalan: Obviously the whole Dalai Lama thing with the choosing of the objects, and all of that stuff—which I love. You know, how they pick the Dalai Lama because he picked the same objects picked from the previous Dalai Lama, so he's the reincarnation of the Dalai Lama. The word Avatar itself is Sanskrit, which is really interesting now [and] because of James Cameron's movie has a whole different implication. There's two different definitions of that word. The Avatar (with the American A) is almost like the cyber version of yourself. And that's the new thing. But the Avatar (in the Sanskrit way) means the embodiment of God in flesh—which is more akin to what Noah plays in the movie. Just that whole idea, and the idea of the elements. When you get married they have the ceremony with the fire and what the fire represents, and then the purity of the water, so the use of elements is huge in the Hindu religion. They put your hands together and pour water on them, and the priest is talking to you about what each of those elements means. It's a big part of our culture.

Question: With the large, choreographed fighting scenes and the graphics, those are kind of new to you and are expected challenges. Were there any unexpected challenges? Anything that you thought would be easy that was difficult?

Shyamalan: We talked about it a little bit earlier (at the breakfast). Not being able to see the movie for so long is a huge challenge—a huge challenge for me. I'm practically an animator in my head. I storyboard, say for a thriller of mine, so that I can walk you through the whole movie. Like a book, I could walk you through it, and then you're just going to put Bruce Willis in it. I redo it, and redo it, and spend months on it. The Coen brothers work like that, and there's a couple other people that work like that. But generally that's not the way people work. I'm used to aiming for a target, seeing it and getting it—great.

So on the day, if this was the scene, I could tell you if we got it and I'd say, "Ya know, Amy's shirt is popping too much. All of that silver, we gotta take that out. This color is way too much, we gotta take that out there. I don't like that that's blank right there. This is not working for me, you need to get me something from set. Let's switch you positions over here 'cause your blue's popping." You know? That I can tell you. But not when we're doing a movie like this, literally all I have is you maybe, and I have to use all of those skills at a later point. I can talk to everybody, all of the crew members, about what I am hoping is there. But you can't even use the thing that I am good at because it's not there yet. But now it's there. Now I'm looking at it and going, "The red in the starburst thing is too bright, pull it out," and they go "great, great, great!"

Now I am back again, but that's like . . . how long ago did I stop shooting? That's a long time to wait to do what you do. I didn't anticipate that. I didn't anticipate how frustrating that was going to be. And then you're so far down the line, and it's so costly. For example, if we were shooting this (the meeting) live-action, you can tell—as the actors and the crew—if I don't think we have it. I'll be tense. "Well, what do you want?" "Hold on, guys, this isn't right. It's just not right. Just give me five minutes and I'll figure it out. Okay, we're taking this apart. We're taking all of you guys out and putting you out in the hallway. It's gonna be a walk and talk while you're getting on the elevator." I don't have that option to do that. By the time I realize I would have done it differently, so much money and time has been spent. There's just no way to tell ILM to start from scratch. It doesn't work like that. So that's a super, super challenging thing. I guess I've learned a new skill of being able to imagine even more in my head and hold to it as long as I can.

Question: So the thriller you keep mentioning, it's not *Unbreakable 2* is it?

Shyamalan: No it's not, unfortunately. I want to do that one too. My favorite part of being an artist is feeling something at a moment, and I can just write it down and talk about what I feel at that moment. Maybe a year later it will seem invalid, and that's why there's such an urge to get it out. I don't feel the way I felt during *Signs*, but I can't have that conversation again. That's the fun part about being an author, you just keep telling your stories. I hope to make *Unbreakable 2*.

Question: Bruce Willis just said he's still up for it.

Shyamalan: Yeah. [*Laughs*]

Question: One of the biggest questions we get on a regular basis whenever we write about this movie is about casting. I'm not sure if you're aware, but there are some fans that have had casting issues with Sokka and Katara, and the Fire Nation. I was wondering if you could finally address those questions and those fans that are concerned about the casting?

Shyamalan: Well, here's the thing. The great thing about anime is that it's ambiguous. The features of the character are an intentional mix of all features. It's indented to be ambiguous—that's completely its point. And so when we watch Katara, my oldest daughter is literally like a photo-double of Katara in the cartoon. So that means that Katara is Indian, correct? No, that's just in our house. And her friends that watch it, they see themselves in it, and that's what's so beautiful about anime. When we were casting, I didn't care who walked through my door. Whoever's the best for the parts, I'm going to figure out like through a chess game. Ideally we separate the nations ethnically—ideally. But I don't know how or what it's going to be. It was so fluid, the casting.

For example, if you found a great brother, but it didn't go with my favorite Katara, then I couldn't use him. Theoretical things like that would happen. There was an Aang that I really loved, but he was like five foot ten. There's all kinds of issues that come to the table. I kept having a board of all the people that I was considering. There was at one time a—I think their background was Chinese—a Sokka and Katara. One of them was a better actor than the other, and I was gathering my pros and cons. "Let's say that was that, what would the Fire Nation be?" And you just do that. Being without agenda and letting it come to the table. Noah's like a photo double for the cartoon; I mean he's literally spot-on. To me, the best part is, I didn't really know their backgrounds. Noah, for me, has a slightly mixed-quality look to him—so I cast airbenders as all mixed race. So when you see the monks and that stuff, they're all mixed. And it kind of goes with the nomadic culture that over the years all different nationalities came to the table. The Fire Nation was the most complicated. I kept switching who was playing Zuko. It was such a complicated and drawn-out thing about practical matters. The first person I was considering for Zuko was Ecuadorian. So I started thinking that way. And then when that person couldn't do it, the second person who came in was much more Caucasian. I was like, "Well then, we have to switch the others. All right, now how are we doing this?" What is the Earth Kingdom was always the issue because the second movie is so dominated by that group, and will represent most of the movie, but it has a small, small part in the first movie. That was important. It just sort of came into being and started to distill.

Dev came into the picture really early on—he had auditioned for me in London. He's kind of like a sweet guy, but he did such a great reading. I always go for the actor. When I was doing *The Sixth Sense*, you literally read the script of *The Sixth Sense* and [Cole's] dark-haired, black-eyed. I always pictured the kid from *Searching for Bobby Fischer* as the lead of *The Sixth Sense*. "We are not casting, hiring any blonde LA kids, okay? Don't even bring them in!" And Haley came in "... You got the part!" How can you not have him play the part? So that's always been my lean. I have hopes of what I want them to be. My hope was that this movie would be incredibly diverse. When we look back on the three movies, without peer, they were the most diverse movies of all time. And that is the case when you watch the movie. It's not like an agenda like when you see a picture of a kid's school with kids on the swings and there's one from each background—it's not like that. It's a real thing. This nation has this ethnicity and when we go deep into that culture, we'll see more and more of that. Again, Dev ended up being my choice for Zuko. I looked for an uncle that could be in that realm. For a moment there I thought of Ben Kingsley. Shaun Toub, who I loved in *Iron Man*, took us into kind of a Mediterranean, Arab and Indian world. I can go as far as that. That would be the breadth of the Fire Nation—that kind of look.

For me, Nicola had a lot of Russian qualities and European qualities, so that's what we're going to go here . . . just like that. Whoever we ended up with, I said that's their nationality. Suki was Jessica, who is a mix of Filipino, and now the Earth Kingdom is going to be all-Asian, so Toph now will have to be . . . like that. There is a sudden [moment] when I looked at the board and I said "this works for me," because I represented everyone. And there's a section [. . .] that's African American 'cause it's such a big country and such a big land [that] I felt you could have some diversity in there as they travel through the different cities there. So, more so than the show, it will have a much more diverse ethnic background. It's not an agenda for me, but it's something I'm super proud of; that when my kids look at, or any kids look at it, they'll see themselves in the movie.

Question: A lot of the fans adore the soundtrack that the Track Team created for the series. Are you planning on including any of their iconic themes for James Newton Howard's score?

Shyamalan: I definitely thought about it, I love the music from the show. James is like my brother, we make movies together and all of that stuff. He and Hans Zimmer did the music for *Batman* and *The Dark Knight*. How we do it is, I show James the script (this is very unusual from other composer/director relationships) and he'll write the themes of the movie prior to the movie being shot. And he does that based on me just yapping away at him, and telling him what I am imagining. The reason I do it that way is because, rather than being diluted, we're all coming from the same pool of inspiration. I'll tell him what I think Zuko means, and what the elements mean. What learning water means to me, you know? That kind of thing. You'll just see him nod and nod. Then he'll go away and write a suite of music. He wrote a suite of music and it's inspired by the show: the drums, the percussion, and things like that. Specifically the answer is no, it won't have the exact themes of the show. It was something we talked about.

But James came up with what I think is his best score of his life. If that's not the best score of the year, I don't know what is. He killed it! I mean he killed it. You heard some of his music in the first teaser that I did. When you see the movie, the music is just unbelievable.

The subject matter is so rich, anyway you want to go, but driven by the emotion. The action is driven by emotion, which is such a great thing for me. We did a little bit of that in *Unbreakable*, but we had a real great opportunity to do that here. One of the great balancing tricks of the movie was, how much Asian influence to put into the patina of the movie. Do you have pagodas? Do you have this sort of thing? The consensus with the production designer and myself, and consequently with James, was it's a flavoring. It's not Asian. We're not in Asia, but it's influenced by it. What medieval stuff is to *Lord of the Rings*, Asia is to us. It's influencing it, but it's not necessarily: that's a kimono or that kind of thing. The same thing goes with the music. We toyed with the idea of it being very *Crouching Tiger*, but we ended up going with its influence, but it has its own world. So I'm really excited for you to hear the score.

Question: What about the lettering? The waterbending scroll is in Chinese lettering. What will it be in the movie?

Shyamalan: That's a really good question. We ended up making up our very own language influenced by Chinese calligraphy. When the characters do their moves at the beginning, there are letters that represent the element behind them. So we have a vocabulary.

Question: Is it a functional language?

Shyamalan: It is. It's all interpretive. They'll take the symbol for water and the symbol for table, and together they mean something else. It might mean someone who is wishy-washy because they don't come from a hard place. We were making it up—what these symbols mean together. When we were analyzing the ones that they used (in the show), it was the exact conversation: it's influenced, but it isn't it.

Question: Can we look for your cameo? Your usual cameo?

Shyamalan: Well . . . [*Laughs*] You know what my kids wanted me to play? My kids wanted me to play the guy who doesn't take a bath—you know, he's too paranoid to do it? [*Laughs*] You're not going to see me in the first one, but you might see me in the later ones.

Question: You mentioned this just a little bit, but will you delve much into the history of the *Avatar* world? And while you answer that question, in the trailer there's a firebender and an earthbender I didn't recognize fighting—is that a historical part?

Shyamalan: No, that's actually the freeing of the earth town that's imprisoned. In the show they did it on a boat, or a barge. I had visited South Africa as I was writing the movie. I visited Nelson Mandela's prison in the rock-quarry and I was just so moved by it. They describe all of the guards standing on the perimeter, and how Mandela was almost blinded by the light off the limestone. So that was kind of the inspiration, a rock-quarry prison. Aang comes in and makes a speech and says: "What are you doing here?" and everybody rises—it's really cool.

Question: What's the other movie in 2010 coming out this year that you can't wait to see? That isn't yours.

Shyamalan: Ohh . . . gosh, let's see. I haven't got [to] see anything.

Question: She [*points to the Paramount publicist*] really wants you to say *Iron Man 2*.

[*Everyone laughs*]

Shyamalan: No joke, I was excited to see *Iron Man 2*. By the way, our final trailer will be on *Iron Man 2*.

M. Night Shyamalan: Seeing Signs

Knowledge at Wharton / 2011

From *Knowledge at Wharton* (December 7, 2011). Reprinted by permission of *Knowledge at Wharton*, University of Pennsylvania.

Filmmaker M. Night Shyamalan fell in love with movies as a teenager and began shooting scenes with a Super-8 film camera. His breakout film, supernatural thriller *The Sixth Sense* (1999), garnered six Academy Award nominations and earned more than $650 million in worldwide box office receipts. Shyamalan is currently in preproduction on *One Thousand A.E.*, a film based on an idea by coproducer and actor Will Smith that Shyamalan will direct. After a recent Wharton Leadership Lecture, he sat down with *Knowledge at Wharton* to discuss trends in the movie industry, his creative process and his future plans.

Filmmaker M. Night Shyamalan fell in love with movies early in life and began shooting scenes with his Super-8 film camera as a young teen. Born Manoj Nelliyattu Shyamalan in Pondicherry, India, he was raised in the US near Philadelphia. His first feature film, *Praying with Anger* (1992), was completed while he was a student at the Tisch School of the Arts at New York University. Following this, Shyamalan wrote and directed *Wide Awake* (1998) and cowrote the screenplay for *Stuart Little* (1999).

Shyamalan's breakout film, supernatural thriller *The Sixth Sense* (1999), garnered six Academy Award nominations, including Best Picture and Best Director, and earned more than $650 million in worldwide box office receipts. After producing *The Sixth Sense* and his three subsequent films—*Unbreakable* (2000), *Signs* (2002) and *The Village* (2004)—in conjunction with The Walt Disney Company, Shyamalan and Disney parted ways over disagreements about the screenplay for his next film, an event documented in Michael Bamberger's book *The Man Who Heard Voices: Or, How M. Night Shyamalan Risked His Career on a Fairy Tale*. Shyamalan ultimately produced that film, *Lady in the Water*

(2006), in conjunction with Warner Bros. and went on to write and direct *The Happening* (2008) for 20th Century Fox, and his most recent film, *The Last Airbender* (2010), for Paramount.

While serving as writer, director and producer on most of his major works, with *Devil* (2010), Shyamalan launched "The Night Chronicles," a planned series of films based on his ideas, but executed by other writers and directors. Shyamalan is currently in preproduction on *One Thousand A.E.*, a film based on an idea by coproducer and actor Will Smith that Shyamalan will direct.

While Shyamalan's films have covered different genres—including thriller (*The Sixth Sense, The Village, The Happening*), science fiction (*Signs*), comic book heroics (*Unbreakable*) and fantasy (*Lady in the Water, The Last Airbender*), they all show a fascination with the miraculous and a sense that the world holds a larger meaning hidden beneath the surface of everyday appearances. In *Signs*, Graham Hess, played by Mel Gibson, asks his brother, "What kind of person are you? Are you the kind that sees signs, sees miracles? Or do you believe that people just get lucky? Or, look at the question this way: Is it possible that there are no coincidences?" As Shyamalan told Knowledge at Wharton, he's squarely in the camp that sees signs, that sees miracles.

Shyamalan recently spoke at Wharton as part of the school's Leadership Lecture series, sponsored by Givology and the M. Night Shyamalan Foundation, where he spoke about both filmmaking and his philanthropic work. Following his talk, Shyamalan sat down with *Knowledge at Wharton* to discuss trends in the movie industry, his creative process and his future plans. An edited version of that conversation follows.

Knowledge at Wharton: Do you recall the moment when you knew you wanted to be a filmmaker?

M. Night Shyamalan: Yes, *Raiders of the Lost Ark*. Even before that, from ten or eleven years old, I [made my own movies] as a hobby, just for kicks. But then at twelve, I saw *Raiders*. The way I saw *Raiders* was fantastic. My friend dragged me. I didn't want to see a movie about archaeology—I didn't even know what that was at the time. It was sold out, and we had to sit separately, which pissed me off, because I was so shy back then. I sat alone. There was an old couple next to me, and they were so sweet. They saw I was a really tiny Indian kid and they got me popcorn and stuff.

Then the lights go [down], the mountain comes [on screen] and then it starts. And I have the greatest movie experience of my life. My jaw was hanging open at the end. Whatever magic Spielberg has, it hit me 100 percent. And I was like, "I need to do this for a living." Then at fourteen, I was at the airport dropping off my grandmother to go to India. I went into the bookstore and picked up Spike

Lee's book *Gotta Have It*, documenting his [early filmmaking experiences]. If I hadn't picked up that book, I don't know if I would have been a filmmaker. It's always these little things that turn you and aim you. [Lee] was from the East Coast and had no family in the business. He just found the way to make movies. And somehow, it demystified it for me. Perhaps that was his intention. And I was like, "I'm going to go do this for real." At fourteen, that was it. There was no way of talking me out of anything.

Knowledge at Wharton: We're seeing the consumption of films change. In the old days, everybody went to the theater and saw movies on the big screen. Now people watch movies at home from a Blu-ray disc or on an iPad. What do you think about this trend, and does it affect how you approach your projects?

Shyamalan: I am an artist whose art form is making cinema for a group of people to watch together. That's what I do for a living. The exploitation of that is unending—but that isn't [what] I do it for. That's not the artist that I am. Someone who makes TV shows is a different kind of artist. The experience of being in a room with 500 people [is different]—you literally share points of view when you watch together.

I once wrote an article about the Nuremburg trial and how these were the worst Nazis in the Nazi organization. These people were animals. And their faces [were like] ice, except for the moment they showed a movie in the trial. When the lights went down and they showed the footage of the bodies being pushed into the pits, their expressions changed and they became emotional. They were watching [the events on the screen] through the eyes of everyone in the theater. They were having a joint experience. They were all connected, and they saw the horror, saw [that their victims] were human beings. And they changed.

That's what I do for a living. All exploitations of that are fine and great, but that's not the tail that leads the dog. And I think, ultimately, as I said in my speech today, that there is a flight to quality right now, because there are so many outlets [for content]. The only thing that has always worked and will continue to work is quality.

Knowledge at Wharton: Is there a tension between getting the funding necessary to get films made and the artistic work that you want to do?

Shyamalan: Well, right now, I'm starting to believe that the future for me, what I want to do—and I know it sounds very hypocritical now, [since I'm] making this giant movie with Will Smith—is to be the Coen brothers and make small movies where I can take great artistic risks and do stuff that I know 30 percent of the audience is not going to dig, because I'm making it for the appropriate budget. I believe the future will be in marketing those movies through social networking avenues, as opposed to just TV—95 percent of the way we sell movies is TV commercials. It will be more of an underground movement.

The world has shifted. It used to be word of mouth only; there was no PA—prints and advertising—budgets. You just put the movie out. *Jaws* just played all year long, based on [people saying], "You've got to see *Jaws*, dude. Let's go see it!"

It's almost coming back to that now. [For example,] let's say I made *The Sixth Sense* for $20-some million, or even less—let's say I didn't use Bruce Willis and made [it with an even smaller budget]. And I put it in five theaters and I didn't advertise. You're telling me, in this day and age, that it wouldn't have caused a ruckus—the first 500 would tell the next 500, and [all of a] sudden it's sold out every show for the next week. And then they're putting it in twenty-five theaters, and those people [tell more people] and so it goes. Because there are so many outlets now [where] we can talk to hundreds of thousands of people any time we want.

So I think it's going to shift. There [are films] that cost $200 million that they have to jam us with because they're not relying on their quality. But then there are these other types [of films]. I've been having a lot of conversations about it changing.

Knowledge at Wharton: But the trend in your work seems to be the opposite. *The Last Airbender* was a fairly expensive film. And *One Thousand AE* is going to be a big budget film.

Shyamalan: It's a big movie. I'm a complete hypocrite right now [*laughs*]. I'm telling you what I *want*. [*Laughs*] Don't do as I do, do as I say: *Make small movies*.

Knowledge at Wharton: To some extent, is what you're doing with the series "The Night Chronicles" more in line with your future plans? *Devil* was made for around $10 million.

Shyamalan: Yes, that's actually the better model. I believe that's the correct model to make smaller movies—and really, honestly, it is my intention [*laughs*].

It's just you get caught up in it. The big movies take longer, so they take me out of the cycle longer to implement these other things. But the trend is there. Even though all you see are *Iron Man*s and *Pirates of the Caribbean*s, there's that whole middle section that's growing [with more modest films] like *The Fighter*, *The Help* and *The Blind Side*, and all those movies that are making incredible amounts of profit for their studios but they're very modest in their budgets.

Knowledge at Wharton: On most of your films you've been the writer, director and producer. Is this because you want to control every aspect of the film?

Shyamalan: Yes. [*Laughs*]

Knowledge at Wharton: Yet with "The Night Chronicles," you seem to be going down a somewhat different path. *Devil* was based on your story idea, but the screenplay and the direction were done by others.

Shyamalan: Right. Yes.

Knowledge at Wharton: Are you loosening up a bit?

Shyamalan: My favorite movie of all time is *The Godfather*. [Director Francis Ford] Coppola, for me, is an utter genius. Coupling him with [writer] Mario Puzo created that incredible, incredible thing. There's great validity in partnerships. As a film director you're, by nature, a control freak. It just is that way. But again, my intention—whether it's fictional or not—is a retreat back to making small, personal visions.

Knowledge at Wharton: You famously walked away from your Disney deal over the production of *Lady in the Water*. Can you explain why? What's the importance of having the studio that provides the funding share your vision for the film?

Shyamalan: You want to believe that person selling it will sell it better if they believe in the product. That's naive, but it's actually what I feel. But that isn't the reality. The reality is the selling departments look at criteria, and they exploit that regardless of what they feel about the overall thing. If you give them these four beats in a movie that they can exploit, they're happy as a clam. They're going to open the movie and make a lot of money. If I made them a beautiful movie that they personally connected to on a deep, resonant level, but I didn't give them the four points, we're going to have a problem.

It was a fascinating moment, because I think the Disney organization was shifting into a different direction. And I was shifting in a different direction. I was trying to be really audacious. I kept taking more and more risks.

I think it was inevitable. Maybe it wouldn't happen on that movie, maybe it would happen on the next movie. Unless I stayed in more of a niche—like, let's say, if I were an action director and stayed in the action genre, and didn't try to do a drama or a mixed genre [film].

I think when I get in trouble is when I do mixed-genre movies, because they're difficult to sell. *Lady in the Water* was the highest audience-rated movie that I've ever done, but [it was] impossible to sell, because there's no genre. Is it for kids? Is it for adults? Is it scary? Is it funny? What is it? And part of me was in the mode of, "I don't want to think crass. I don't want to think how to sell it."

[Making that film] was for me, as an artist, the favorite moment in my life. I ended up making it for a wonderful man named Alan Horn at Warner Bros. I think he related to the emotion of the piece. But I'm friends with all those people who were working with me at that time, and all the tension that existed when the breakup happened is gone. I'm friends with all of them now. They're at different places themselves. And it's nice to know that the friendships still continue.

Knowledge at Wharton: What determines the success of a film for you?

Shyamalan: If I can I look myself in the eye and say I was artistically truthful.

Knowledge at Wharton: You also seem to want to have an impact on a large audience.

Shyamalan: Yes, [but] it's not a calculated thing. I know that sounds hard to swallow. My favorite thing to eat is a cheeseburger. My favorite athlete is Michael Jordan. My favorite TV show is *Seinfeld*. I'm not tacking towards popularity—these are my tastes. When I'm doing something very personal, it just happens to also be appetizing to a large group of people.

For example, with [*Black Swan* director] Darren Aronofsky, whom I love, what's personal to him [speaks to] a much more narrow group of people who will deal with that kind of darkness and angst.

I genuinely think everybody is great. I really am a positive guy. You don't have to tell me to make it feel good. I do feel good, so I tend to write stories like that. And so it ends up having a large impact. And that's just a nice side thing.

There are moments when I'm not like that. [While making] *Unbreakable*, I was darker, and I ended the movie darker. Sometimes I feel that way. With a [film with a] dark ending like *The Happening*, it was going to be difficult to hit certain [revenue] figures. But there's always a voice that seems at least momentarily accessible to people.

But it isn't ever the box office numbers or anything like that. I definitely want my partners to make a profit. It also helps me creatively. For example, on this sci-fi movie I'm doing, I'm using artisans who haven't done big movies. I have that ability to do that because of the previous box office, and they trust me to make the correct decisions, to take the correct risks. I get to do interesting things with the costumes and the sets and the lighting with these interesting, amazing artists, because of the box office thing. So there's a nice protection that happens from that, which is, hopefully, self-fulfilling.

Knowledge at Wharton: You mentioned in your talk that one of the things you're still working on is handling criticism and not taking things personally. Some critics have been pretty rough on you at times.

Shyamalan: Yes.

Knowledge at Wharton: How does that affect you? Does that change the way you go into your next film?

Shyamalan: It really wouldn't bother me because my aspiration, as I said, isn't necessarily acceptance. But I always want to understand what's going on. What are the principles behind the tension or the miscommunication? I want to totally get that. Then I can choose not to react to it, or react to it. My constant, in self-analysis, is to try to figure out: Am I complicit in this situation? How did I create this situation? What is my role in it? Do I want to continue that role? Do I want to change the course of that role?

As long as I understand it, I'm much more comfortable with it. And I feel I'm in a strangely decent place of wanting that amount of passion [people] have when they speak about the movies, and the expectations. My obligation is to figure out the bridge so that I don't just let go of me and please them. That would be disaster.

Knowledge at Wharton: In your talk, you mentioned Alfred Hitchcock and pointed out that some of his films—like *Psycho*—were not critically well received at the time. And, of course, looking back on them now, we take a very different view. Do you think the same will happen with some or all of your work? Will people look back on them and take a different perspective than they took when they were playing as first-run films?

Shyamalan: I hope so. I want movies that have long shelf lives and that do better as you look at them out of their particular context. I've seen [the trend] moving in a positive way in the different movies, so I'm happy about that.

Knowledge at Wharton: In *Signs*, the Mel Gibson character asks his brother, "What kind of person are you? Are you the kind that sees signs, sees miracles? Or do you believe that people just get lucky?"

What kind of person are you?

Shyamalan: I just watched that last night. Definitely the miracle. I'm a miracle man. [*Laughs*]

Knowledge at Wharton: You said you recently saw *Signs* again. Do you often rewatch your earlier films?

Shyamalan: No. I have this thing with my kids—on their birthdays, they get to watch one of my movies. When they see them for the first time, they have to be screened for them in the way that they were intended. They watch them in movie order, as I made them.

The middle child got to watch *Signs*. It was her birthday. She's been really excited for a whole year, waiting to see *Signs*. Next year she'll see *The Village*.

Knowledge at Wharton: What advice would you give to young filmmakers trying to get into the industry?

Shyamalan: Work on your authenticity, your own voice. It's true for everything, not just moviemaking. Know yourself. Hone your point of view with the people you're around and the experiences you have. Be attentive. A rich, specific and unusual point of view is going to be very successful in any film.

The Shyamalans: An Exclusive Interview with the Main Line Power Couple

Melissa Jacobs / 2014

From *Main Line Today* (July 24, 2014). Reprinted by permission of *Main Line Today*.

M. Night Shyamalan looks noticeably at ease on the cushy moss-green couch in the barn-turned-bungalow that doubles as his office. The space has a living room, a kitchen with a dining table, an antique-ish wooden desk, and walls lined with framed posters of his many films.

And it's a safe bet the Oscar-nominated writer/director spends a lot of time on that couch. It's positioned in front of sliding-glass doors that overlook a vast, grassy, markedly empty area on his Malvern property—just grass and sky as far as the eye can see. The setting is pure Shyamalan. *The Happening* and *The Village* contain this motif, as will *Sundowning*, his upcoming release, which was shot in the Main Line area.

Sundowning is a serious departure for Shyamalan. The independent film was cast with unknown actors and shot on a tight budget. Shyamalan is also making his first foray into TV with *Wayward Pines*. The ten-episode supernatural thriller airs on FOX next year and stars Matt Dillon, Juliette Lewis and Terrence Howard.

It's not as if Shyamalan *has* to go indie at this point. Despite a lukewarm critical reception, 2010's *The Last Airbender* grossed more than $319 million worldwide. And last year's *After Earth* brought in over $243 million. Yet the "it's not as good as *The Sixth Sense*" comments continue to dog Shyamalan. In typical Philadelphia fashion, he's at once embraced and criticized.

Shyamalan, who turns forty-four this month, has been making a lot of surprising career turns of late—perhaps none more so than *I Got Schooled*. Part memoir, part manifesto, the book chronicles his research into possible solutions to the public education crisis afflicting so many of our cities. To many people, the book came out of nowhere—and not in a spine-tingling or suspenseful way. After all, what does an Episcopal Academy graduate know about urban education reform?

More than you'd think. For the past thirteen years, he and his wife, Bhavna, have been quietly and consistently funding the work of education-focused nonprofit groups around the world through the M. Night Shyamalan Foundation.

Targeting reform, Shyamalan has spent the past six years meeting with experts, checking out high-performing schools, and poring over proposed efforts. His goal is to convince voters and legislators to make policy decisions based on raw data—not opinions or anecdotes.

Meanwhile, back on the Main Line, his children attend private schools. And that brings us back to the question posed to Shyamalan at the start of this story: "Are you asking me why I care about this group of people?"

Well, yes—and the answer has a lot to do with his father. Shyamalan was an infant when his parents immigrated to America from India. They came to Philadelphia for a reason. "My dad chose Philadelphia as the beacon of America," says Shyamalan. "When I watched the miniseries *John Adams*, I was weeping; I also wept reading Adams's biography. It's the American dream, and I'm very aware that I'm a product of that because I had the educational opportunities that my parents provided."

Inner-city parents can't provide the same for their children, and Shyamalan sees that as an unacceptable compromise of American values. He also understands that this inequity has been a reality for so long, and seems so overwhelming, that people are tired of hearing about it.

Shyamalan, of course, wants to change that. As for his wife, she wants to change the world.

Bhavna Shyamalan arrives at Burlap and Bean Coffee in Newtown Square on a cool spring day. Dressed for the weather, she's wearing leggings and an oversized sweater—a typical Main Line mom outfit. But Bhavna is no trophy wife. Quiet and a bit shy, the NYU graduate has a PhD in clinical psychology from Bryn Mawr College.

Though she's never sat down for an in-depth interview about her work with the M. Night Shyamalan Foundation, it's immediately clear that she's driven by its mission to provide educational opportunities for those in the poorest, most desperate parts of the world—especially girls.

Created in 2001, MNSF's initial focus was offering financial support to American families that adopted orphans from India. Bhavna found an orphanage to work with, and that became the model for MNSF's future partnerships. "We don't need to reinvent the wheel," says Bhavna. "We just need to make it turn."

MNSF has since implemented multiyear partnerships with organizations in India, Tanzania, Guatemala, South Sudan, Nicaragua, Kenya, Ghana, and Liberia. Around here, they work with Philadelphia's Springboard Collaborative and other local groups.

Bhavna and MNSF executive director Jennifer Walters-Michalec vet the leaders of these nonprofits in extensive interviews. The two travel to each location, staying for several days. "We stay in tents or huts, usually without indoor plumbing and sometimes without beds," Bhavna says. "We eat stew or soup and some bread—whatever everyone else is eating—and we bring protein bars," Bhavna says.

Born in India, Bhavna was raised in Hong Kong before the family came to the US in 1986. She attended a private high school in Hong Kong and planned to go to an American college.

Her mother had different ideas: "She thought that being too educated would hurt me—that, for women, malleability was an attribute."

But Bhavna was fortunate to have her father as an ally. "He believed in the value of education, even for girls," she says. "He wanted his legacy to be that he provided educational opportunities for me as well as my siblings."

When Bhavna was accepted to NYU, her mother relented—but not without a few conditions. Bhavna worked two jobs to help pay for tuition, and she had to live at home so Mom could keep an eye on her. And she certainly wasn't allowed to date.

Bhavna's parents had an arranged marriage, and her mother expected Bhavna to do the same. So when she finally told her parents about a fellow student named Manoj Shyamalan, it didn't go well.

An aspiring filmmaker? Forget it.

She married him anyway. "I said, 'How much money he makes isn't important to me. I have an education. I can work,'" Bhavna recalls.

After they married in 1993, Bhavna put her undergraduate psychology degree to work in a clinic, counseling young victims of sexual abuse. While her husband wrote screenplays, they lived off of her paycheck. "It actually felt good—not to him, but to me," Bhavna says.

To ease the financial burden, they moved into Night's parents' home in Penn Valley—specifically, his sister's old bedroom (pink walls and all). Bhavna was accepted into the Bryn Mawr graduate program and Night kept writing.

"It was a struggle, but I didn't mind that," says Bhavna. "The times that I feel the most strong are when I go through a struggle and come out of it. Because then I know I can do it."

In the late nineties, when Night began to experience some financial success with his screenplays, the Shyamalans bought a condominium in Chesterbrook. "It was one of our favorite places to be," Bhavna says. "We had our first two children there, and I liked all of us being close. We had a little office with a sofa bed. Late at night, I'd study, and Night would come in and sleep on the sofa bed just to be near me."

Later, the Shyamalans upgraded to a house big enough for their growing family. There they got the call that would change their lives: *The Sixth Sense* screenplay had sold—and Night would direct.

The film grossed more than $600 million worldwide and snared two Oscar nominations. "But *The Sixth Sense* didn't change my life," Bhavna says. "Having children changed my life. And meeting poor, uneducated, abused children around the world has changed my life. What *The Sixth Sense* did was give us the ability to change the lives of those children."

The screening room at the Shyamalan home is outfitted with maroon fabric, dark wood, chandeliers and rows of cushiony chairs.

"I'm not used to doing this and I'm kind of shy, so forgive me," says Bhavna, shielding her face with the bundle of papers she has in her hands.

At this small gathering of friends and MNSF supporters, Bhavna is introducing Katie Meyler, founder of More Than Me in Liberia. An overwhelming number of Liberian girls are forced into the sex trade because they have no job skills, no money and no education. To help change that, Meyler has set up a free school for Liberian girls. Bhavna and Walters-Michalec visited last year, and More Than Me is now one of MNSF's many beneficiaries.

"I'm asking you to care about people you've never met in a country you've never visited," Bhavna says. "But I have to tell you that I left my heart in Liberia."

Those in attendance donate a large sum of money to More Than Me, and the Shyamalans match it. The money will provide scholarships for fifty-two Liberian girls enrolled in the school.

Bhavna was shocked when several girls involved in the More Than Me program recently reported being sexually assaulted by a teacher. The man is now being prosecuted, and Bhavna is proud of the girls for coming forward; this, she believes, is the epitome of empowerment. For the students' sake, MNSF will continue to support More Than Me.

By all indications, Bhavna is just getting started in her new, more public role with MNSF. The goal is to generate awareness and funds for well-deserving nonprofits around the world. And she hasn't been wrong yet about any group she's championed. She's got a sixth sense about these things.

How to Master the Supernatural

Matt Blake / 2015

From *FHM* (September 2015). Reprinted by permission of Matt Blake.

It was first heard this side of the afterlife by a village psychic in India, while reading the palm of his father, Nelliate C. Shyamalan. "He looked at his hand and said, 'Your name will be known across the Seven Seas,'" says Night. "My dad's reaction was, 'My God, I'm going to commit a crime, that's the only way.'"

The doctor didn't commit a crime. Instead, he emigrated to the US with his wife, Jayalakshmi, their infant children Veena and Manoj, and set up a clinic in Philadelphia. But he never forgot the mystic's words.

"He would look at his name on the sign above his surgery and say, 'This must be the name!'" Night goes on. "But whenever local kids sprayed graffiti over it—as they did everywhere—he'd scrub it off and say, 'This cannot be it.'" He spent the next twenty years searching for a sign. But none came. "He's watching, waiting for his name while, all the time, his son is messing about with his Super 8 film camera," Night chuckles. The camera was the key. And, in 1999, it finally came true . . . with a twist.

"I remember my father getting out of the limo at my first premiere, and there, on the billboard above the red carpet, were the words, 'A film by M. Night Shyamalan,'" Night says. "He turned to me with tears in his eyes and said, 'It happened . . . it finally happened.'" That film was *The Sixth Sense*. It became one of the highest-grossing films of all time, received six Academy Award nominations, and left a generation of moviegoers unable to piss at night without thinking of Mischa Barton vomiting all over their bed. It instantly turned Night into a "name-on-the-poster" filmmaker. His father's name was finally known across the seven seas.

The film's success couldn't have been a more appropriate beginning for the twenty-nine-year-old film director, who would not only become Hollywood's master of the supernatural, but also its king of the twist. If you haven't seen *The Sixth Sense*, you probably know the surprise (mostly when you realize Bruce Willis once had hair). With his next three movies, Night made the "shock ending" his calling card. He followed *The Sixth Sense*, a spine-tingling ghost story about a boy who "sees dead people," with superhero suspense-drama *Unbreakable*, alien-invasion mystery *Signs* and psychological thriller *The Village*. To date, his films have raked in more than $2.7 billion at the box office. He is one of the highest-paid writers in Hollywood and one of the most prolific directors of his generation.

"My wife would say I've lived a charmed life," he smiles. "Basically, it's always been easy, she would say." And what about Night? "I would say I wouldn't have it any other way," he replies, rather cryptically. "I just want to be true to myself. That's not to say I haven't personally felt . . ." He pauses for a moment. "Moments of great darkness. Our industry's good at giving you those."

We're with Night in a generic London hotel room. His mop of black hair is framed by light from the open window behind him. The trees outside whisper something about the Hollywood Illuminati enslaving us all. Possibly. Or they just rustled in the breeze. It's so difficult to tell. Anyway, Night's started talking about Rubik's Cubes.

"All I wanted to be when I grew up was a Rubik's Cube champion," he says. "I could do it in forty-five seconds, without looking at it." Trouble is, freelance Rubik's Cubing isn't the most lucrative of jobs. So he became a filmmaker instead. Manoj Nelliate Shyamalan was born on 6 August 1970 in Mahé, India, before his family relocated to an affluent suburb of Philadelphia, Pennsylvania. At the age of nine, he stole his dad's 8mm camera from a cupboard and began spoofing the films *E.T.*, *James Bond*, and *A Nightmare on Elm Street*. By the time he graduated from high school, he had made forty-five short films and once told his guidance counsellor, "Making movies is not only my hobby, not only my primary interest, not only my extracurricular life; it is my future."

There, he also shortened Manoj to M and turned Nelliate to Night. Calling himself Night was a bit like calling a tall guy Tiny: there is nothing of the night about him. He is sunny and smiley. But at work, he plays the devil with light and dark. "The unknown is what makes things scary," he tells us. "The why, how, what . . . that story is more frightening than 'blood-dripping-down-the-wall' horror. I like the unknown presence that causes fear and takes you back to a childlike state. Plus, it's much cheaper to film." Childhood is a recurring theme in Night's films: It's the kid who sees dead people (*The Sixth Sense*), or talks to aliens (*Signs*), or bends airflows (*The Last Airbender*) or is a talking humanoid mouse (*Stuart Little*, which Night wrote but didn't direct).

"It's funny," he says. "When I write, it's always children. There is something pure about the moment a child loses their innocence. When they become aware of their surroundings, but are still uncorrupted by the complexities of adult life."

What about Night's own childhood? He has many times thanked his upbringing for his success—even now, he regularly calls his mum, a retired gynecologist, for life advice (she only lives twenty minutes down the road from his home in Philadelphia).

"My parents are really funny, really classic immigrant Indians," he laughs. "They came to the US when it really wasn't that popular to be an Indian doctor. They taught me that when you dream with enough clarity, and work hard, things manifest."

"This will give you a sense of what they're like," he laughs. "Once I said, 'President Clinton wants me to come to dinner.' My mum was like [*puts on an Indian accent*], 'This is great! Maybe something good will happen!' I said, 'No, mum, that is the good thing. The president wants to have dinner!'" He laughs heartily: "In their mind, immigrants are always trying to achieve; like, 'Maybe the president will give you part of the east coast!'" Did he? "No," says Night. "He just said he liked my movies."

The shaft of light behind Night's head has moved with the sun. Now it's cutting through the room like at the end of *Ghost* (not one of Night's films) where Demi Moore can see Patrick Swayze for the first time before he spirits into the afterlife. But unlike Swayze, we're not letting Night out of our sight; we want to know more about that darkness.

"Hollywood gives you a feeling of not knowing your own value," he says. "It does it to all of us. Take Robin Williams—I was so saddened by his passing, partly because I never told him what he meant to me. I'm sure in his skewed version of things he thought he was of no value. But the industry does that to you. It tells you your worth, whether that's zero or a billion."

This is a sensitive subject to broach with Night, for he knows as well as any director how it feels to be pounded by the press. While the box offices have banked him millions, the critics have not always been so kind. His 2010 outing, *The Last Airbender*, for example, made more than $530 million in cinemas but was deemed so bad that it won five Razzies—trophies given to movies judged the year's biggest stinkers.

The *Wall Street Journal* dismissed his 2008 film, *The Happening*, as a "woeful clunker." The *Telegraph* branded *The Last Airbender* as "a man-mountain of dung." *The Guardian* called *After Earth*, starring Will Smith and his son Jaden "a triple-whammy of abysmal acting, directing and story." That must have really haunted him.

"All [the critics] can touch is your ego, and that shouldn't be there anyway," says Night. "Crush it and then what's left is something pure; the pure artist," he ponders. "That's how you should be, on a good day—the most comfortable version of yourself." We speculate that nobody can take that kind of beating without feeling bruised. He backtracks. "Yeah, only sometimes I feel that way," he concedes. "Other times I feel like, 'Ah, this is so unfair, this is ridiculous. They're treating *Alvin and the Chipmunks: The Squeakquel* the same way as my movies and there's no way [that's a better film].' I shouldn't let it affect me as much as it does, but I'm human. It's such a public thing."

What stops him dusting down his old Rubik's Cube? "I was on a show recently with Steven Moffat, the creator of *Sherlock*," he says. "He was asked if he made shows for the audience, and replied, 'No, I don't even know what to buy you for a present; I would totally screw it up.' He was so right—we don't know what people want, the only thing you can do is make something pleasing for you."

So screw the audience? "No. I guess the best answer for me is that if I can reflect myself as a human being in my making of movies, then I'll be happy. I have strong convictions creatively that I can't bend for anybody. On the other hand, I do care about people; it's important for me that you're okay and that we're connecting." Isn't it tiring having to constantly fight against Hollywood's cigar-wielding ringmasters with dollar signs for pupils? "I feel sad when I see a movie from a filmmaker that I respect and I can tell they toed the line," Night tells us. "But that's what this business does: it just hurts us."

His words conjure up images of Hollywood as an evil organ grinder bent on beating his troupe of depressed movie monkeys into snapping their clapperboards in time with his tune. "The supernatural thriller was the dance I first danced with everybody," he says. "So they want that date over and over; or, at least, the system wants me to dance that dance—I don't know if the audience wants me to always do that."

Indeed, *The Sixth Sense*'s ending proved so sensational that, not only did it earn the movie those Oscar nods, but [it] spawned countless copycat thrillers, each trying to outdo the last (with diminishing returns). *Unbreakable*, *Signs* and *The Village* also had "gotcha" endings, earning him a reputation as the Twist King. He became so good at it that the only possible plot twist his audience wouldn't see coming was no plot twist at all. So that's exactly what he did.

"Coming off *The Village*, I had a sense of, 'Do I really want to make another movie with a twist, back-to-back?'" he says. "No. I'll go do something different."

So, in 2006, he made *Lady in the Water*, a modern-day fairy tale about a man who finds a water nymph in his swimming pool. It bombed, making only $98.6 million from a $95.8 million budget. "It was one of my favorite experiences, and my least successful movie," he says. "But the handful of people that saw it, it [became] religion. It was religion to me, too."

A weaker director might have considered hanging up his clapperboard in the face of such a beating. Not Night. He issued a bespoke form of payback on his critics: The hack in the movie gets eaten by a monster. "If you don't put one foot into an area that scares you, you're not doing it correctly," he says. "There's no way around that. You're an artist, you have to make yourself vulnerable. If you don't, you're not an artist."

Still, when Hollywood's helter-skelter does all get too much, Night has the medicine: 182 chest-beating minutes of pure, bellowing Mel Gibson. "I pop in *Braveheart*," he says. "That's my go-to 'I feel like beating somebody up' film. It's a male fantasy to have something so fierce inside you that you can take on a country. For me, [the movie] is the line that I strive for—like the kind of giant commercial movie that studios think of, but that has depth and is so effortlessly itself. It just so happens to be a total cheeseburger as well."

In fact, Gibson starred in Night's movie *Signs*. They're mates. "It was lovely when I worked with him," says Night, with a smile. So he's not like what we see in the media? "He was an incredibly sweet guy, a hard worker; we couldn't have been any closer," Night says. "He was like a big brother to me."

We decide it's best not to pull on that thread too hard. Anyway, our time together is almost up. The trees have stopped whispering and the clouds have moved over the sun, casting a spooky shadow across the room. But Night is still as bright as ever.

"My advice to anyone getting into the business is: Don't try to be me, you'll lose. Don't try to be someone else. Be yourself. Always yourself. If you can be exactly that, you have a strength that's so specific, it's incredibly powerful." That's where lies Night's core heroism—in his ability to stay true to his principles in spite of criticism. There's one question left to ask. He's made a career of giving us the heebie-jeebies for the best part of fourteen years, playing musical chairs with our most basic existential fears. But what frightens M. Night Shyamalan?

"I just want to tell my stories, that's all," he says with a smile. "My only fear is that I won't be able to tell them to anybody, that they won't be able to hear me or that they won't get it. That's the scariest story I know."

Given how well his career is going, that would make for an unexpected twist.

"The Only Thing That Matters to Me Is What I Think about My Own Films"

Gauthier Jurgensen / 2015

From *AlloCiné* (October 7, 2015). Reprinted by permission of *AlloCiné* and Gauthier Jurgensen.

Gauthier Jurgensen: *The Visit* is a self-produced film that cost five million dollars. It's your lowest budget since *Praying with Anger*, your first feature. Does this allow you to keep complete artistic control?

M. Night Shyamalan: Yes, definitely, and it was a better fit for me. It was a way to make a film without worrying about the whole commercial aspect. It allowed me to focus on a new tone and enjoy the moment, as if we were making a film for a small festival, with the audacity that goes with it. Characters/story, story/characters, that's all that matters. You get that in your head and see what happens.

Jurgensen: With *Sixth Sense* or *Signs*, you made a name for yourself in horror cinema. You were even nominated for the Oscar for best director in 2000. Why did you turn to family films afterwards (*The Last Airbender*, *After Earth* . . .)?

Shyamalan: For my children. They were that age! I didn't have kids when I was making *Sixth Sense*. Or maybe they were young. In fact, I've always done both, since in parallel to *Sixth Sense*, I was writing *Stuart Little*. You could even say that my "thriller" side started with *Sixth Sense*, since my first two films were family films. And now, my children are teenagers, so I'm back to making horror films. They even ask for them! In a way, *The Visit* is right up their alley. In fact, I had them read it and they loved it! So here we go again. We're getting back into the dark movies. If I have one more child, I will have to make family films again [*laughs*]. We'll do *Stuart Little 3*! [*Laughs*]

Jurgensen: It seems that there has been a falling-out between you and the public for the last ten years. How do you react to this systematic bashing of your work by the public and the critics?

Shyamalan: It's their right, everyone is free to react as they want to what I do. The important thing is how I react. The important thing is to remain dignified.

If I answer with kindness and love for the cinema, it will be felt. And then I don't have to spend my energy on whether people will like me or not. It always shows when you do it. What I'm most happy about is when I get my characters right. I think that's the case in *The Visit*. And then we'll see: maybe as the films go on—and I may make another forty, who knows!—all this great story will sound pretty accurate. The first thing I heard about *Unbreakable* was, "I hated it." Nowadays, people often tell me: "I love it, it's a classic!" Which one should be given credit? Neither, of course! You have to follow your instincts about the films you make. You stick with it and then you move on to the next film, and so on. None of this is going to help or discredit the next story you tell, but you have to go for it: it's a new adventure. Do that every time and you'll be fine because you'll have integrity and you'll have spent your energy properly.

Jurgensen: *The Visit* is still very reminiscent of *The Sixth Sense*. Are you nostalgic for that period when everyone adored you?

Shyamalan: That's all fiction to me. I'll tell you how I lived it: when *Sixth Sense* came out, I opened the *New York Times*. They were shooting me down. I closed it and went on to write *Unbreakable*. *Sixth Sense* got mediocre reviews, wasn't mentioned once in the awards, until the Oscars, when suddenly it was nominated. In fact, most critics didn't see it until it made $150 million at the box office. That's when the art world magically began to embrace it. Then there was *Unbreakable*, which got mixed reviews. It's one of my lowest box office scores. The only film to finally be unanimously applauded was *Signs*. Then, *The Village* was hated, and here we go again. In fact, when you think about it, my two films before *Sixth Sense* were not even released in theaters! There's a big gap between what you think I experienced and what actually happened to me. I recently came across a list that included *The Village* in the top twenty-five films of the 2000s. I'm very happy that people change their minds like shirts, but again, the only thing that matters to me is what I think of my own films.

Jurgensen: *The Visit* is your first film in found footage. How did you manage with this genre, you who like so much the meticulous framing?

Shyamalan: Everything was planned to the millimeter. All my shots were composed. I make a real distinction between documentary and found footage. Found footage is random, ugly and cannot be art because it prevents the mise en scène. Whereas documentary, I can find a beautiful light for it. I can give it a dramatic tension. There is a point of view behind it. It makes a big difference! I had to make the film beautiful from the point of view of a very talented fifteen- or sixteen-year-old girl trying to make a film about her family. I tried to give it a lot of grace. It just came together for me, because I'm used to composing each of my shots. In this case, I thought about them a little beforehand, when I was writing the script. That's the only difference with my other films.

Jurgensen: In *The Visit*, we find some of your signatures, which we would like you to comment on. The first one is the representation of young extra-lucid teenagers that you have been directing since your second film: *Wide Awake*.

Shyamalan: It is not conscious. I like adolescence because it is a rather sad age. These young people stop believing, they give up, they become like us. They become normal and they discover that the world is what it is. But it wasn't just that for them before: they believed in everything! At least, that was my case when I was a kid. And telling stories about teenagers who say, "Wait a minute, this isn't right," gives me the opportunity to portray characters whose eyes are opened and who understand that there's more to life than we think. Like the little boy in *Unbreakable* who says to his dad, "I think you're a superhero," or those kids who say, "There's something weird about Grandma and Grandpa." I really like to use that moment in growth.

Jurgensen: You also often feature elderly people who become mute, incoherent, violent and even suicidal, as in *Sixth Sense* or *The Happening*.

Shyamalan: Yes, this is the taboo subject that is at the heart of *The Visit*: our fear of the elderly. We don't talk about them much in society, we cut them off . . . They go to institutes and we hardly dare mention what they go through there, because it disgusts us. It's probably our fear of dying that makes us see them as ghosts. For me, it was a major subject, never really addressed until now. We always react to it with humor, disgust or fear. I remember when I was shooting *The Happening*, I thought, "I could make a whole movie about that old lady!" She was really scary. I remember staging her in a doorway with a nightgown over her. She was terrifying, but I didn't understand why. Because she was just an old lady! She couldn't hurt us. In truth, it comes from us: it's this fear of dying.

Jurgensen: You often introduce in your films a character who knows more about cinema and the development of a story than the others. Is this an incarnation of yourself?

Shyamalan: [*Laughs*] All the characters are me, in a way. A version of me, at least. The two teenagers in *The Visit* are really two sides of me, anyway. The older one is an aspiring artist who loves and respects film and has a very auteurist point of view. She sees everything from the sacred perspective of her camera. The little boy, on the other hand, is a joker who just wants to be entertained. He has no idea about cinema, which is not like me. But I like to entertain, make people laugh and react.

Jurgensen: There is also a film critic in *Lady in the Water* and a little girl who guesses what will happen next thanks to the ghostly presence of her mother in *Signs*.

Shyamalan: Yes, and even in *Stuart Little 2*, by commenting on the way the stories are made, we were creating a mise en abyme. Yes, I like to hint by introducing a story within the story. The art of storytelling, I find fascinating. So, I think of the film critic in *Lady in the Water* who discovers that he is a secondary character and that he is probably going to die. He's hoping that it's an all-ages movie, with no nude scenes, which would give him his only chance to survive! [*Laughter*]

Jurgensen: In one scene in *The Visit*—which was later cut—you see a figure on a roof in the distance. This is a recurring figure in your films. It recalls the alien in *Signs*, or the suicidal workers in *The Happening* . . .

Shyamalan: It was a moment in the film that we cut, indeed. The girl is shooting scenes around her grandparents' farm. She looks back at the house and sees someone standing on the roof, looking like he wants to jump. She's scared, she sees this figure in the distance and says, "Isn't that grandpa up there?"

Jurgensen: You've made much more expensive films. Have you ever felt that the film was getting away from you?

Shyamalan: It often does, naturally enough, because there are hundreds, if not thousands, of people working on big budget films. There are many complex layers, that's the nature of these projects. It's hard to remain an author in these cases. At the end of the process, there's a guy behind his desk who's going to design your shot, which is going to cost $100,000. You can ask to rework it, but for a small change the bill goes up by $8,000. And if you want to change it again, it's probably another $4,000. And if you want an additional animation, it's $25,000 . . . It's really quite different.

Jurgensen: What about the sequels to *Unbreakable* that you were considering at one time, for TV or for the theater?

Shyamalan: It's true that I thought about it. Viscerally, I don't like sequels. I don't like that little comfort, nor do I like people to have expectations about what they're going to see. It's not my thing and it doesn't make me want to write. But if I can find a new way to make this movie and an original story to make it stand out from *Unbreakable*, I might consider something.

Jurgensen: Did you ever feel like you missed the superhero era with this movie?

Shyamalan: Yes, I did. [*Laughs*] It was too early! At the same time, it's more of a comic-book drama than a comic-book adaptation. We didn't even use it to brand the movie because no one thought that comic books in movies would interest anyone. And now, we're not getting out of it!

Jurgensen: You say that each of your films has a theme. What are they?

Shyamalan: For *The Visit*, that's easy: forgiveness. That's why the whole film is about redemption, about not being forgiving enough, and about these kids who don't understand that they have to forgive their father. They think they are making a documentary about their mother to make her forgive their grandparents. But after the rage, pain, emptiness, confusion and hell they cause throughout the film, they discover that it is actually up to them to forgive. And when I understand what my film is about, I deduce what each scene should look like. *Unbreakable* developed the idea that everyone has a role to play in life. When you're not in tune with your role, you always end up being unhappy. As for *Signs*, it was about the existence of a whole. Is there a grand design? Are we part of a gigantic enterprise or does nothing make sense? Does life have a purpose or will we all end up being abducted by aliens? In which case, it doesn't matter if your wife is run over by a car or if Martians invade the planet . . .

Jurgensen: What is your favorite movie in your filmography? And in this film, what is the scene you preferred to shoot?

Shyamalan: I immediately thought of *Lady in the Water* when you asked your question. There is a scene where four sisters are holding each other by the shoulder. It's a kind of ceremony where the hero, Paul Giamatti, becomes aware of his role in the story. He starts talking to his family who have disappeared, telling them, "I miss your faces, they make me think of God." I love that line, and the way the sisters put their hands on him to give him strength. It's a ceremony that I think is beautiful.

Jurgensen: You are preparing a new film with Joaquin Phoenix and Jason Blum. Can we know more about it? Is it going to be scary?

Shyamalan: Yes, it's a thriller.

Jurgensen: *Wayward Pines* is successful. Will there be a season 2?

Shyamalan: I'm optimistic. I can't guarantee it. I'm still figuring out the story, where I want it to go and where I want it to end. Anyway, I don't want to stick with it until I know the ending. Everything has to be thought out in advance. I know that TV doesn't work like that. Usually, you start a season as soon as the previous one is successful. But I don't want to do that. I don't like to see episodes on TV where we repeat ourselves, where we don't make any decisions and where we stall because we don't know where we are going. For my show, I want to know exactly what our axis will be, if we do it in ten episodes or in twenty and how much time we have. It will be done like that and not otherwise.

M. Night Shyamalan Interview: *Split*, Nonconformity, Creative Freedom

Ryan Lambie / 2017

From *Den of Geek* (January 17, 2017). Reprinted by permission of Ryan Lambie.

Following the expensive Will Smith sci-fi vehicle *After Earth* in 2013, M. Night Shyamalan returned two years later with lean, found-footage horror thriller *The Visit*. Made for a tiny fraction of *After Earth*'s investment, it marked something of a turning point for the writer-director: tense, quirky and at times blackly amusing, it was Shyamalan's lowest-budget film since the nineties, and also his most warmly received piece since 2002's *Signs*.

The partnership between Shyamalan and prolific indie producer Jason Blum—who's also taken such filmmakers as Barry Levinson, James DeMonaco and Damien Chazelle under his creative wing—is clearly an effective one, since the two have reunited for another movie, *Split*.

Starring James McAvoy as an unpredictable kidnapper suffering from dissociative identity disorder, it sees three abducted teenagers attempt to negotiate their captor's numerous personalities and find a means of escape. Unsettling and tonally unpredictable, it's prompted a further uptick in Shyamalan's critical notices, and provides an effective showcase for his strengths as a crafter of suspense. Likewise his cast, with McAvoy chewing into his multiple roles with evident hunger; *The Witch*'s Anya Taylor-Joy, who plays one of the kidnapped young women, is arguably his equal.

On the eve of *Split*'s UK release, we met with Mr. Shyamalan to talk about the making of *Split*, the creative freedom afforded by partnering up with Jason Blum, and why Yorgos Lanthimos's nightmarishly strange drama *Dogtooth* blew him away . . .

Ryan Lambie: Congratulations on the film. I liked the sentiment that traumatic experiences, and scars—whether physical or mental—can become a beneficial part of your personality.

M. Night Shyamalan: Mm-hmm. Yeah. The conversation was about the things that happen to us, that change us—is that bad? Is it always true that being normal is the right place? That nonsuffering is the way of life, you know? I think Casey's character [played by Anya Taylor-Joy] feels that as well: she feels detached from everyone because she feels so different. She's had a different experience. These kind of healthy girls that she's with, she can't really relate to them. They're not mean—they're actually really nice. It's the flip of a [conventional] horror movie— normally, they're bad girls who are having sex and doing drugs, so they get killed. It's a flip in this movie: you're in a life-threatening situation because you're good. I was explaining this to everyone; "These are the nice girls."

Lambie: That's interesting. I hadn't thought of it that way. [Casey's] a nonconformist, isn't she? I might be wrong and getting old, but I sometimes feel that society's becoming increasingly conformist. You have to act, look and dress a certain way to be considered successful and popular.

Shyamalan: Oh yeah. I agree. I was in Madrid yesterday, where we had a screening at a university, and it was packed. The kids were all losing their minds. I was saying, "All we have, to alter the world, is our point of views. No matter whether you're a doctor, an artist, a journalist, whatever—it's about your point of view. So cultivating a specific, honest, new point of view is [important]. If you're walking, talking and acting like everybody else, and you have a general point of view, you have no value to the world."

"Whoever, in this room," I said, "is the most specific with their point of view is going to be the most powerful. So don't just think the same way as everybody else."

It's so hard, though. I don't know how old you are, but we didn't grow up with the pressure that these kids have. I mean . . . how old are you?

Lambie: I'm thirty-nine, so I was around way before social media and stuff, so . . .

Shyamalan: Yeah. So the blessing of going in your room, and there's nothing in your room but the shit you put in there, right? So there's something belonging to your girlfriend here, and there might be a baseball mitt over there. It's not like we just sit on our phone and looking at all the same videos and having all the same interactions. We have moments where we can just be ourselves. It's kind of fascinating, given the film's subject matter of compartmentalizing, right?

Lambie: Right, yes. Do you think of yourself as a nonconformist in terms of filmmaking?

Shyamalan: I know my instincts are counter. I get most excited when I'm doing something that hasn't been done before. Whether it's the truth or not, it's a feeling I get. I feel heartache if something feels similar to something else. So in that way, yes. Last night, before we got on the plane to come here, I just ran to the Prado, the museum. There was a guide there who was taking me around, and he was explaining how there are these painters who shattered what happened, and there was a constant swing between classicism and then shattering it. And then it lost its power and swung back to classicism in order to relearn the basics, and learn to reinvent them again. It's almost like a movement of artists—not that they all got together and said this, it just happens. It made me really inspired. I'm going to make this next movie . . . [*trails off*]

These were the thoughts in my head: why did *Dogtooth* blow me away? What is it that they were doing? What was it that went on in that movie that [made it so effective]? There's something there, you know? Why am I drawn to this, why am I drawn to that? Really go for it. Really dig, dig, dig, you know? It inspired me to think like that. Because it's so easy not to; it's so easy to generalize. It's less work, but not as satisfying.

Lambie: Do you think that's what you did with *The Visit* in a certain way? You stripped everything down, shattered it, in terms of formal style, and made a found footage, documentary-style movie.

Shyamalan: Yeah, yeah. For me, I feel excited by that challenge. It's almost the reverse of, if you gave me $200 million to make a movie, I'd be so lost. I love the feeling of, if you said, "Alright, everybody gets a small amount of money to make a movie. Go make the best movie you can." I'll be like, "Yeah! Let's go." [*Rubs hands eagerly*]

It's so exciting. I don't know what it is about that, but limitations really excite me. I don't trust myself with excess—I'm a minimalist. I like limitations: "You have to have the script done by this point. You have to shoot it in this many days. You have this money." I like it.

Lambie: So working with Jason Blum has given you the chance to experiment, then, within that smaller form.

Shyamalan: You know, it's really funny. Jason Blum's really prolific with his company. I make these movies, and I ask Jason to come on as an advisor. So I showed him *The Visit* after it was done—not completely done, but about 85 percent done. For me, what I look for in a producer isn't to tell me how to shoot or all that stuff. No one's ever involved in all that stuff. What I like is, "Here's what I'm worried about. What's your opinion? I'm worried about this; I'm trying to do this—what do you think? Should we show it this way."

And then it's, "Here's the movie, what do you think? Oh, you thought that part was slow? Great, great. You liked that? Great."

He's more like a big brother advisor. And I love [Jason Blum's] tastes. He's super calm, and he calms me. He gets me in my better head space, so I'm not being defensive. It comes from confidence—so, for example, we showed *Split* four months before it opened, right? We open next week. We showed it, I think, in September, in Austin, Texas, at a film festival. It's crazy to do this, with a movie with the ending that it has and all that stuff.

I said [to Jason Blum], "This is what Universal is suggesting. They love the movie, and they want to put it out there in the world that there's something special coming. And there's a huge chance that we're going to hurt our movie here. A huge chance. What do you want to do?"

So Jason and I talk it out, and I trust him. He comes at me and goes, "We got the goods, man. Just be confident. Go in there and just trust it. It's not a guarantee, but let's trust it." If I don't have that big brother there, I probably don't make that move. I come from insecurity. But it worked out for us, and it could have not worked out for us, but it did. Either way, it was still the right decision. That's a perfect example, though, right? A big giant decision like that—you don't want to make it in a vacuum. Jason and I, I love us as a team, and I hope we make more movies together. I'm lucky to have found somebody that champions original filmmaking like that.

Lambie: That's the interesting thing looking over your career, is that you haven't done any sequels or remakes. So it's important for you to have that control.

Shyamalan: Here's what I'd say: there's an optimal process for me. That process looks like this: I want to take the pressure off the original shoot. Like, with these two movies: if I could lay out my dream version of a movie [production], well, I just did it twice. I'm going to go for it, and shoot as fast as I can, but know I'm coming back. And so in my schedule, I have everyone scheduled to come back three weeks later—every actor, every crew member comes back for three, four days. I don't know what we're shooting, but everyone's coming back.

So think about that. You took the test, you got to look at it really quickly for three weeks—you don't get a really in-depth look, but you get to look at it. Then you go, "This scene doesn't work for me. God, I know we can do that better. You know what? I didn't want it to be angry, I wanted it to be this." Those kinds of things. So slowly you build up what you want to shoot, and the schedule gets filled up. You tell all the actors, "This is what we're shooting." Literally, right up to the day we're filming, I'm still filling it up with things. Those three, four days get full, so you automatically get a second rewrite before it's done. And it's not ever really done, because in these two movies, the other things I did in the process was, I kept the sets up the entire time. So they broke down . . . I think it was in November. So just, like, three weeks ago, I took the sets down.

Because I was, like, "Wait, wait. I need that, I need this." And because we made it at a certain level, and because all the material's there, and because everyone comes to the table—from James [McAvoy] all the way to the PAs, they all know the deal here. This is how we're making the movie, and if I come up with a great idea, they trust me, and I trust them. If I say, "I'm working on the movie, can you spare me a Saturday? When can you come back? Great. Come to Philadelphia, and we'll grab that scene." You know what I mean? That fluid movement allows me to do what I do when I write a screenplay, which is a listening process. Both these films have allowed me to hone it, and that's the process that's the most important. And yes, with that came "I have an idea" and I can just execute it. There's no committee, there's no checking, there's no nothing. I just go ahead and do it.

Lambie: It's interesting how you balance the fear we have for the antagonist and the empathy we have for him. This reminded me a lot of *Peeping Tom*; I don't know if that was an influence.

Shyamalan: I don't think I've seen that.

Lambie: Michael Powell, 1960.

Shyamalan: Ohhh, yeah, yeah. I haven't seen it, but I know of it. Is it great?

Lambie: Oh, yeah, yeah. You could watch these two films on a double bill, I think.

Shyamalan: You know, I'm gonna write that down right now. [*Gets up and fetches a pen and paper from a desk nearby*] No, my favorite thing is getting film recommendations, because when someone asks me, "What's your perfect day?" My perfect day is, I read a book, I work a little bit at home, very quiet, and then I go down to my theatre and watch a great, classic movie, like a gem.

Lambie: That movie was interesting, because it sparked a real moral outrage at the time, precisely because of its empathy for the villain. And I wondered if you were aware that going out on a limb like that can be risky.

Shyamalan: Yeah. So in a traditional narrative, you probably don't want to sympathize with the antagonist. The structure of the movie is, "I'm going to simultaneously raise the stakes and make you more sympathetic of the antagonist," right? Really interesting challenge. But that is the disorder: the disorder is, there are many people in the room, and some of them aren't great. But most of them are great, so now what are you going to do? My big question, that I love, is: Someone with DID is holding a gun on someone—can you shoot them? Because you're not just shooting one person, you're shooting, in this case, twenty-three people. Are you going to extinguish twenty consciousnesses when only three are really capable of immoral acts? If you truly believe this, that the mind and body are different consciousnesses, you can't. It's a really powerful idea.

Lambie: It is, yes.

Shyamalan: And then you could jump . . . I don't want to get all philosophical, but one could argue that's why you can't kill anyone.

Lambie: I was going to say that, because human beings are complex. We're not just one person.

Shyamalan: There's something that could get you or I to commit a crime. There's something. Family, or some outrage, or jealousy—we can't pretend, you and I, that we couldn't get to that point. So should we be extinguished because of that part of ourselves? There's a real argument there, then, for not killing anyone.

Lambie: Absolutely. Did James McAvoy ever voice to you whether there was one particular persona that he was nervous about portraying?

Shyamalan: You'd have to ask him. I'm blurring now what the challenges were, because it was all so challenging. For me, I have a tone in my head and I'm trying to get it. Who's Patricia? We do something like twenty takes of her coming in the door, and I'm like, "There it is, right there. That one where you did the thing with the eyes." She's a fanatic, right? And her fanaticism makes her forget that other people are not on the same page as her. She thinks, "This is so beautiful, what's happening to you three. It's so beautiful that you're a part of this ritual. And I am equally offended with Dennis touching you. That's completely wrong—completely wrong. I mean, I'm angry."

Once he gets that vibe, that's her. Righteous! And blind to the notion that this might not be what these girls want.

Lambie: I think a lot of people will be asking you about James McAvoy's performance, but I think Anya Taylor-Joy's performance is the anchor in this film. She really is amazing.

Shyamalan: Thank you so much. She is. She's very raw. I really relate to two kinds of actors, which is, the highly trained, technical actor . . . I can just be, like, "I didn't buy what you just did on the fourth line. You moved from there to there, and I don't buy it." And if they try to fight me, I'll say, "I didn't buy it. You think about it: you made an emotional jump that you didn't believe in, so let's talk about it." And they have all the technique to go [*mimes the act of moving small boxes around very quickly*] and do all the prep. I can push and push and push.

Then there are the newbies, who are just open and raw. I can do the same thing, and they're hyper-sensitive to everything I say. Anya was hyper-sensitive, just like kids are. So you have to be gentle with them: "When you made that decision, you were not defending Casey. So you came off as arrogant there. Is that Casey? Because I didn't write her that way. She's not meaning to hurt these girls." That kind of thing. And you might see her tear up a little bit, because she's like, "I didn't mean to portray her like that." It suddenly becomes a real thing that they empathize with. And the kids—I consider Anya a kid even though she's just turned twenty—there's this pure empathy that these individuals have.

And of course, most kids don't have that, so when they audition, they have already learned all the tricks that you and I have. Like, "I'm just pretending to be this person." Because we learn so many pretending things as adults, we don't even realize it. Even that [*adopts a note of false delight*] "Hi!" Everyone does that, and that's fucking not real, right? What we, you want is, in a truthful moment, I see the person that I recognize, and I'm slowly building up an emotion. That's the proper level of speed for our emotions: "Oh hi. Great, nice to meet you."

Lambie: It's falseness. Again, it's creating a persona, isn't it? It's wearing a mask.

Shyamalan: Yes. Yes, it is. It's really fascinating, the stuff we're talking about.

Lambie: Like I said, I like the way your films go out on a limb. You don't do the obvious thing; you don't take the easy way out in your storytelling. So what is it like for you, emotionally, when an audience doesn't necessarily connect with one of your movies? I'm thinking about something like *The Happening* or *The Last Airbender*.

Shyamalan: Well, you shouldn't really look at the result, even if the result is great. That shouldn't be where the energy goes. The people that I've loved in art, both in movies and in literature, they're not looking at that. You can smell when I'm trying to please you. And if they're trying to please, they're not artists. That's the definition of a prostitute: prostitution is the selling of a value system. So if you did something that you love, and in the moment it was misunderstood, that's all good. My energy should be in "Did I do the very best version of those characters? Did I understand those characters, or did I round the corners? Was I lazy? Did I rip out my soul to get to them? Was I truly honest with myself in uncovering these characters?"

If you put the energy there and tie it to that craft, it will work out. I don't know the form of how it'll work out, it may not mean that I open at number one with every movie, but it will work out. Because people will say, "There's no way around it. He has a very clean value system that he believes in." I've learned over the years to not put my energy into that: "You're an idiot! You're a genius! You're an idiot! You're a genius!" Don't put any energy into that; the only thing that matters is the story and the characters. And again, everything will work out if you do that. If I spend the next thirty, forty years until I'm an old man concentrating on that, I'll be happy. If I spend my energy on, "They love me, they hate me, they love me, they hate me," I won't be happy.

Lambie: With that, we're out of time. M. Night Shyamalan, thank you very much.

Superheroes as a Disease of Cinema?
M. Night Shyamalan Interviewed about *Glass*

Matthias Hopf / 2019

From *moviepilot.de* (January 17, 2019). Reprinted by permission of Webedia and Matthias Hopf.

It took almost two decades for David Dunn, played by Bruce Willis, to don his superhero cape for a second time and move through nighttime alleys to save people from evil. In *Glass*, the unlikely savior is not only confronted with his old nemesis in the form of Samuel L. Jackson, but also faces the beast that James McAvoy brought to life three years ago in *Split*. This encounter was orchestrated by none other than M. Night Shyamalan, who as director and screenwriter already brought the two previous films to theaters. Last November, we met with the filmmaker for an interview and asked some questions about the long-awaited crossover.

Matthias Hopf: Hello, how are you?
M. Night Shyamalan: Hi, I'm doing well.
Hopf: With *Glass*, the merging of *Unbreakable* and *Split* is now coming to theaters. But was *Split* intended to be part of the *Unbreakable* universe from the beginning? What was the process/development stages?
Shyamalan: I knew [when producing *Split*] that I had written a few scenes beforehand. I like to outline individual things and sometimes I'll write a little bit of dialogue and a few moments to get a feel for it. I had these [ideas] back in 1999—specifically Patricia, Dennis, Hedwig. I knew then that they were going to be characters, those three. I didn't know anything else. And I also had no idea what the beast was. There was always talk of a beast, but [in my drafts] they never got to the crucial point.
Hopf: Why did it take so long for the *Unbreakable* universe to return to theaters?
Shyamalan: It's because I tried to make stand-alone films for a long time, until I devoted myself to smaller, more restrained films. That's when I suddenly

realized that the story of the second film, *Split*, was hiding in one of those small, scary films. As a result, I decided to tell the story as a thriller with a character who has kidnapped three girls and has multiple personalities. Now the girls have to manipulate the different personalities to escape.

Hopf: It's an entertaining story that incessantly announces the arrival of a beast until it finally makes an appearance. It's a little crazy—who or what is this beast?

Shyamalan: But it was this strange tone of the story that I liked and wanted to explore more. So I worked out the drafts and went to Disney and said, "Could I . . . maybe . . . [refer to *Unbreakable*]. If they hadn't given me permission, I would have just done *Split* as a thriller. But in the end, everything was perfect.

Hopf: Over the years, there have been many rumors regarding an *Unbreakable* sequel. If you had made the film earlier, in the early 2000s, what would it have looked like? Is there still some of that potential sequel at the core of *Glass*?

Shyamalan: It probably would have been a much more elaborate film, both in terms of the size of the story and the budget. If I had made it right after that, that's probably what would have happened. But now I make smaller, tighter films. I probably wouldn't have made a thriller then that surprisingly turns out to be a sequel. Probably the Beast would have been the main character and Bruce [Willis's character David Dunn] would have found out who was behind it. I had to rethink all that for *Glass*. [*Laughs*]

Hopf: You've already shot blockbusters with budgets in the millions. For a few years now, that's no longer the case. Do you miss making films with big budgets?

Shyamalan: The only films that were really expensive were the two I didn't write. Those were the film adaptations . . . *After Earth* and *The Last Airbender*. The rest had moderate budgets. I've always been a cautious filmmaker about that. But now I'm taking it a step further. I won't get paid unless the film is in the black. The actors have all waived their usual fees. If the film is successful, they will share [in the profits]. It's a very different mentality. All the money [$20 million for *Glass*] is on the screen. Now it's very small budgets.

Hopf: Since *Unbreakable* hit theaters, we've seen a glut of superhero movies. Franchises like the Marvel Cinematic Universe are getting bigger and bigger. How does *Glass* fit into this landscape of superhero movies?

Shyamalan: Because *Unbreakable* came out before all these films, there's a lot of commentary in *Glass*. The film comments on that evolution.

Hopf: Can you give a specific example of that?

Shyamalan: You have to see the movie for that, but it's definitely going to comment on what's happened in the past few years, with all these movies that everyone is obsessed with all of a sudden. So it's not just comic book adaptations that are being addressed, but also the society that can't seem to get away from them. So I get to reflect a lot in *Glass*, which is a lot of fun.

What *One Flew over the Cuckoo's Nest* Has to Do with *Glass*

Hopf: Sarah Paulson's character says the pithy line in the trailer, "The three of you are convinced you have special abilities, the kind you see in comic books. I've developed an effective therapy for this kind of disorder." Are superhero movies the disease of contemporary cinema?

Shyamalan: [*Laughs*] The theory in the film is that society has become so obsessed with comic books that a disorder is created. The disorder is "you think you're a superhero." Now there's a whole wing in a hospital that treats people who think they're characters from a comic book. In the past, that would have been pharaohs or an Egyptian deity—now you think you're Aquaman or Superman. Now you have to go through therapy. Just because you think you're good at swimming doesn't make you a real Aquaman.

Hopf: Do you think there are any real heroes at all?

Shyamalan: What interests me is the possibility. Let's look at one of the diseases featured in the film: Osteogenesis imperfecta [colloquially known as brittle bone disease]. That's the disease where your bones are very, very fragile. That's given by nature. We know it exists. So, by nature, the opposite must also exist. But if you have the other version of this disease, you wouldn't know it. If you were in a car accident, you wouldn't hurt yourself, you wouldn't break your bones.

You'd think you were lucky. Right. Never broken a bone, never seriously injured: You play football and you'd always think how lucky you were. You probably wouldn't even really think about it. Right? But if that person decided to fight crime, they wouldn't get hurt like others. That was the premise of *Unbreakable*. Are there heroes? Are there superheroes who may not even know they are superheroes?

Hopf: Is there anything in particular that inspired you while working on *Glass*?

Shyamalan: A filmmaker?

Hopf: Yes, or a book, a piece of music, a movie.

Shyamalan: Oh gosh, there's so many things, but the biggest inspiration was definitely *One Flew over the Cuckoo's Nest*. That's the biggest influence on *Glass*. I love that movie. It's one of my all-time favorite movies. Both the setting and the structure and the way the characters talk to each other and the quirky humor and the scary facets were extremely influential on *Glass*. Mike Gioulakis [the cinematographer on *Glass*] and I also watched a lot of Robert Altman films. We love Robert Altman.

Hopf: Which one in particular?

Shyamalan: *3 Women.* The structural compositions alone! We've both watched a lot of Robert Altman films for *Split.* That's why there are some zooms to discover in our films, long zooms.

M. Night Shyamalan on the Staging and Editing of His Films

Hopf: Speaking of staging: Your films often feature far fewer cuts than is the norm in many other films currently besieging theaters. Instead, you invest in long takes. Why is that so important to you?

Shyamalan: That's a fantastic question. It's aimed at exactly what I love about cinema. So that should go a little deeper now. It's about what it means to cut. What would happen if we were shooting a scene and I do your take first, then mine, then yours again, and finally mine again? We could spend the next thirty minutes asking that question.

[*Editor's note: To help you understand the following paragraphs, I briefly define three important terms: A shot is the smallest cinematic element, so it shows what the camera captured from the time it was turned on to the time it was turned off. Meanwhile, several takes can be made of a shot until it is in the can with the desired result. The sequence of several takes revolving around one event is then called a scene.*]

Let's say we would shoot a scene together and, let's say, take 6 was the best. You did something and I reacted to it and it was just beautiful, really authentic. But what if we had shot the scene like this? First a take of you, then of me, of you, and then of me again. So take 6 would have been just one take of many, regardless of who was in front of the camera at the time. Let's say your close-up would have been take 6. Then we would come to me and in the editing room we would have to do a third version of that scene, which would then be only half take 6. The other half is the take of me.

Consequently, the original take 6 will never exist in the film. The moment when we were connected in front of the camera never exists in the film. It's lost. If you don't think of such scenes in one take, then exactly those precious moments are lost and you create another moment in the editing room. So we could have shot the most beautiful take 6 ever, but it wouldn't have ended up in the finished film. Once we cut your take 6 and my take 8 together, we create a third version that is neither take 6 nor take 8, but something completely new. So the final performance is made later in the editing room.

Hopf: The magic happens less on the set than in the editing room these days?

Shyamalan: Exactly, we create the scene later by adding an after-the-fact reaction on my part. That's not the reaction I had when we first shot take 6.

Hopf: But isn't editing a crucial process of filmmaking?

Shyamalan: It's definitely the direction in which filmmaking has evolved. It used to be different, though, because editing was more difficult then, and it wasn't digital either. The art form back then was "do it here [on set]," and that's why I try to do everything I can to capture take 6 in all its glory and let the audience share in experiencing that exact moment.

Hopf: Can you imagine shooting a film completely without editing? Or what about *Birdman* and its invisible cuts?

Shyamalan: I love that, but that would be something completely different. Sooner or later, a cut is necessary. The cut is a reboot, like a blink. There's a book called *In the Blink of an Eye* [by Walter Scott Murch]—have you read it? It's all about editing. If I say to you, "Hey, what are you doing," and then I blink, I have a new thought. One minute I had one thing to say, but then the next one pops into my head like an image, "Oh, I had a fight with my girlfriend."

Cutting is important because it's violent. Film is a collection of images, so it's important to cut them together. It's just crucial not to overuse the power of editing. So it's always a compromise between wanting to keep take 6 and yet not giving up the rhythm of cutting. Both tools are there to be used, but should not be overused disproportionately.

How the Colors in *Glass* Tell Their Own Story

Hopf: *Unbreakable* featured an interesting change of colors. David Dunn's scenes were first in bluish-greyish tones, while Mr. Glass appeared in yellow light, before the colors were switched in conjunction with the characters. The teaser posters for *Glass* also work with color coding for the characters. What's behind that?

Shyamalan: If we were shooting a scene here, it would be noticeable that the room is saturated with traditions, and there are some primary colors. But what stands out the most for me is this light green. That says something to me, it's really interesting. And then there are these shades of pink here that throw me off a little bit, but the color is important. It's crucial. Are you sitting in a light green chair with a gray sweater for a reason? Are you trying to tell who you are with it? Are you trying to hide who you are? Those are the big choices here. I chose green for David because the color represents life.

The hero wears the life-giving green. It's associated with life-giving qualities, the emergence of life. It's a biological thing. We associate green with life. Purple, on the other hand, represents something royal. We associate it with monarchy, with queens and kings. That's also how Mr. Glass sees himself—as one of the most important people in the world. The ocher of the beast, which is perhaps also a bit mustard-colored, comes to me from monk's robes. There's something religious and spiritual about it. For me, the beast is a prophet. It converts people, sees itself as an evangelist. "Listen to me"—this is exactly the type of beast. That's why he has these colors. The evangelist, the king and the hero.

Hopf: You shot all your films on 35mm film before moving to digital with *After Earth*. How did that decision come about?

Shyamalan: When you shoot CGI films, it's very difficult [to shoot on film]. It's very complicated and increases the cost tremendously. With *The Last Airbender* and *After Earth*, I was hired to shoot the films that way. With *The Visit*, the digital is hidden in the nature of the film. The story is told by two kids with a video camera—you can't shoot that on 35mm film. That's what the story dictates. With *Split* and *Glass*, it's entirely due to financial reasons. It costs $500,000 more to shoot on film.

But those films are smaller and have a much smaller budget. So those were decisions that [cinematographer] Mike Gioulakis and I made. We both love film. However, there are very few labs and technicians left who can develop film. And even fewer assistants who know how to work with film. It's very difficult . . . and is disappearing more and more. At the same time, digital cameras are improving, also in terms of mimicking certain textures that we like so much. Also, digital allows us to shoot longer at night with low light sources. That's also an advantage.

Hopf: Would you still consider switching back to film?

Shyamalan: I love film and am actually considering going back to film for the next project I'm working on.

Hopf: What is the project in question?

Shyamalan: It's a series for Apple. That's where I'm thinking about it right now. We're doing test footage and then we'll decide.

Hopf: Will you direct all the episodes of the series?

Shyamalan: No, just the first one and maybe one more later in the season. So maybe two, but not all ten episodes.

Hopf: And beyond that, are there plans for a sequel to *Glass*? Or an entire *Unbreakable* Cinematic Universe?

Shyamalan: No, I don't think so. That's the end of it. You know I like standalone movies the best. But I also never say never. Because maybe one day I'll have another great idea. But now I don't see it. After all, it took me eighteen years to make [*Glass*] [*laughs*].

Hopf: I would wait the next eighteen years, too, for whatever.

Shyamalan: [*Laughs*] Thank you!

Hopf: And thank you very much for this long interview!

Shyamalan: Thank you very much!

M. Night Shyamalan Reflects on the Evolution of His Career, His Filmmaking Philosophy, and That *Old* Ending

Steve Weintraub / 2021

From *Collider* (July 30, 2021). Reprinted by permission of Bradley Davis and *Collider*.

With *Old* now playing in theaters, I recently landed an extended interview with writer-director M. Night Shyamalan about the making of his latest film and career. During the wide-ranging and very fun conversation, Shyamalan talked about his favorite movies, collecting first edition Hitchcock posters, what he's learned during his career that he wishes he knew early on, why working with lower budgets has been his secret sauce, what happened with his *Labor of Love* script that was originally going to star Bruce Willis, how *The Sixth Sense* changed during the writing process, why *Split* has so many deleted scenes, the way he directs on set, meeting with Steven Spielberg to write the fourth *Indiana Jones* movie, and more. Of course, we also talked about the making of *Old*, how he charted the age of every actor for every scene, how he came up with the *Old* ending, and more.

Steve Weintraub: What movie do you think you've seen the most?
M. Night Shyamalan: Either *Raiders of the Lost Ark*, or *Jaws*, or *Silence of the Lambs*. They're all fighting. We just watched *Silence of the Lambs* again, so it's still ticking up.
Weintraub: When you watch movies like that, do you ever as a director—'cause I've spoken to some directors and they've talked to me, or they've mentioned that they've taken notes or they've written down shots or whatever, have you ever watched any of these films and written down something specific that you want to incorporate into something you want to do?
Shyamalan: I don't want to say I always take notes, but I often take notes watching movies. I just have a pad next to me. Always try to learn something. I'm

very much lost in the story, but if something cinematically hits me, I'll scribble it down on the piece of paper next to me. If I'm at a certain point in the making of a movie, especially the writing, the latter stages of writing, like the last third of the writing process, I'm very careful about what I watch because that's super, super influencing me.

Weintraub: Do you have a favorite sci-fi or fantasy film?

Shyamalan: I mean, so many. When you said that I went to *Alien* right away, just as soon as you said that.

Weintraub: If you weren't writing and directing, what do you think you would have done?

Shyamalan: Now, I would say I would love to have opened a bookstore and have a small bookstore, but that's more of a fantasy retirement job than I guess my alternate career. I guess I would have been a doctor, right? I mean, that's what my parents are, all my uncles and aunts are. I think I would have probably been odd bedside demeanor, probably telling stories to the patients, but...

Weintraub: Is there anything that you collect?

Shyamalan: Fantastic question. I do collect posters. I'm running out of wall space because I don't like to have them kind of like hidden anywhere. I have first edition Hitchcock posters in my house.

Weintraub: Do you have the huge ones?

Shyamalan: No. The one sheets. So you put them in there, all the one sheets from the original, including *Rebecca*, which is a very rare first edition to have of that movie, which I love that movie.

Weintraub: Have you posted any pictures of the posters?

Shyamalan: I should. I should actually. It did cross my mind that I should do that wall of those.

Weintraub: Yeah, absolutely. Because I want to see them. What TV series have you watched all the way through, more than once?

Shyamalan: I'm wondering if that actually exists, that I did do that. I've been toying with going back to watch *Sopranos* from beginning to end. I've been toying with that. I mean, you're not counting *Friends* and *The Office*, right? You're not counting that, that doesn't count. That's perpetually on in everyone's house all the time. That doesn't count.

Weintraub: Here's the thing, though, that does count because you can say, "*Friends* is always on," or, "*The Office* is always on," so that does count.

Shyamalan: Yeah. I think the trilogy of *Seinfeld*, *The Office*, and *Friends* I think is on. *Friends* is more of my daughters and my wife that they have it on top all the time. Rachel's doing something in our house at all times.

Weintraub: What do you wish you knew earlier in your career that you've learned as you've made all your projects?

Shyamalan: Wow. What a great question. The thing that at times makes it dissonant in its immediate consumption at that moment, that thing, is not necessarily a bad thing, and oftentimes is the wonderful thing about it that makes it resonate and makes its brothers and sisters, the other films, even more seen in a stronger light. So for example, that *Signs* was my biggest opening movie is because of *Unbreakable*, that kind of relationship of the dissonant movie to the next movie. Something that I've learned over time is, it's a very strange thing to do art and commerce together like that, and I've been so lucky to have this long relationship with the audience and the ones that has created this bond are the dissonant ones that has that, just that weird thing about them. And so, I would tell my younger self, because I tack towards that. My instinct is that to do that dissonant thing and to follow that, to just, don't worry about being the popular kid on the day.

Weintraub: People used to go to see a Hitchcock movie because it was a Hitchcock movie. Now people go to see a movie because of your name. When did it hit you that like, "Oh, my God, my name is actually getting people into a theater"?

Shyamalan: I don't think I've quite internalized that entirely. It's weird to pass a billboard or something. We went to a wedding, the first thing we did is after the pandemic, the first thing, we went to a friend's wedding, and it was in Baltimore. And, drove up, and got out of the car, come into the hotel and all the bellboys had the masks on. And they were like, "*Old, Old!*" And they were all yelling it out and I'm like, wow, this is wild that they're coming, they're interested in the author. Then, went into the Starbucks, and the guy at the Starbucks was like, "July 23rd, man, July 23rd." I was like, wow, this is, it's amazing. I take it very seriously, the relationship of the craft of it, that relationship. It's one that we have with authors of novels. It's one we have with authors of plays and it's more rare in the movie industry. Just a blessing, dude. What can I say? I mean, my movie's opening up in movie theaters in a few weeks here, and the first one that went all over the world in 1999. So it's like, man, it's amazing.

Weintraub: What you don't know about the story you just told me is that the employees at the hotel and at the Starbucks were all given $5 each by your wife to say these things.

Shyamalan: Is that right, is that right?

Weintraub: I just want to keep—

Shyamalan: By the way, it would work the other way. My wife would be like, "Here's $5 not to say . . ." "Just don't tell him it. Don't remind him he has . . ." "Here's $5. Just don't say it."

Weintraub: You've worked with all different budgets. And I'm curious if you find working with a lower budget is almost more . . . I don't know, it's easier. Not because it's less money, but because it's almost less responsibility, the people paying for the movie. And if it doesn't work, it's not the end of the world. Can you talk about what it's like working in these different budget levels?

Shyamalan: Yeah. I mean, for me, it's been the secret sauce, to do these four movies and make them at a very low number, the lowest I can make it for. In that relationship with my partners, I can deliver the most unique and provocative product, which I think is our weapon to be different. The more different it is, the better it is for us in the marketplace. That's my thesis. But I'm being responsible. It's a very interesting thing. We're trying to do something anomalous, like say releasing *Old* in the summer. And honestly, every movie that's out's at least 10 times the cost of the movie, right? It does give me comfort, it allows me to do very provocative things, darker things. I don't have to feel like I have to play it safe. I can be very dissonant, like we were saying, and know that for the most part we're going to be okay. We're building a relationship that the studio and I love with the audience. It's a very special thing, dude, that's going on. I don't mind doing it this way. In fact, I love it. And in fact, to other filmmakers I would say, you should make your movies for the lowest number that you can have freedom, that should be your goal. There's an equation for that. The moment you take the extra dollar, you have now committed to something other than "I'm going to listen to these strange voices that are telling me, 'Slow it down,' or, 'Kill this person,' or, 'Have this . . . ,' 'Shock them in this way.'"

Weintraub: This question I ask to a lot of filmmakers, but I think you're in a different position because I think a lot of people want to be in business with you, and if you came up with an idea, but . . . if you could get the financing for any dream project, what would you make and why? And I'm not sure if this question applies to you, but let's see.

Shyamalan: I don't know if it applies to me, because that's exactly what I'm doing. I'm trying to think. Is there a movie to finance that . . .

Weintraub: Like I said, this might be a question that doesn't apply to you because as I said, I would imagine everyone wants to be in the Night business.

Shyamalan: Well, you bring up an interesting thing. Say there was a big franchise movie, right, that I was like, "Wow, I'm really interested in this because it has an opportunity, but I want to do the small version of that," and that has happened. I won't say what movie, that has happened. It has crossed my mind. "Wow, I would be interested to do the $18 million version of that, if everyone was willing to do that," and it crosses my mind, but then it becomes, that particular IP is so important to that studio or that company, that risking it in that way makes no sense. Why would you try to invent it in that way? There's actually been, I think, three of those situations where I was like, "Hey, I'll do the really down-and-dirty version of that," so it's the reverse a little bit. It's almost like, "Will they allow me not to take the money, and not to spend the money?" Do it in this way. But then the ramifications of that are limitations that I believe in that are positive. Let me ponder more. Maybe I can think about it. But yeah, it's weird, because that is what I'm doing, right? I'm financing these movies that wouldn't be able to be financed in the studio system, traditionally.

Weintraub: Do you have a lot of scripts in the desk that have never been made?

Shyamalan: No. I wrote one in college that I almost made at the time, and then I made the other movie for Miramax at that time, but there's only one since then that I've written that . . .

Weintraub: Are you talking *Labor of Love*?

Shyamalan: Yeah. *Labor*'s there, there's actually two, if you add. There's one more that I have another idea for that I may make one day, so there's two.

Weintraub: Whatever happened with *Labor of Love*, I think you were going to do that with Bruce Willis?

Shyamalan: Yeah.

Weintraub: What happened with that one?

Shyamalan: It's emerged so many times in my career. A couple of times with Denzel. It's just a drama. It's not a thriller, it's just a drama. It's something that I wrote. It's a romance, essentially. It was the first thing that I wrote that actually brought me into the industry in a real way. It was so long ago. So, it means a lot to me. It's very emotional. At this point, it's almost a period piece, because it was set in 1993, '94. It won't make any sense now with cellphones and everything that we have, smartphones, and so you would either literally have to do it as a period piece now, from that time period. It's very meaningful to me. It almost feels like a novel or something that I wrote. Trying to know when to do it and how to do it has always been on my mind. It's a very meaningful piece.

Weintraub: Which of your films went through the biggest change from your first draft on the page to what people saw on screen?

Shyamalan: Great question. Man, let's see. My initial reaction is *Sixth Sense* because that was the one that started out as just a straight crime. There was no therapist, it was a serial killer movie when I first wrote it. It was a crime scene photographer, was the main character, and his child sees the victims of the serial killer. So, that was the original idea that I had in my head.

Weintraub: Which of your films do you think had the most deleted scenes?

Shyamalan: Wow. Great question. That's that one, I'd be guessing, I would be guessing at, because that's a tricky one. I'd have to see. I have all these cards for each scene when you're editing and then as they go into the graveyard, as they come out, they go into this pile that I call the graveyard that list goes. I'm thinking it's *Split*. I'm thinking it's *Split*. That had whole storylines that came out, a character that came out. The first cut of that was like three hours, so it was big.

Weintraub: I apologize for not knowing, but do all of your deleted scenes end up on a Blu-ray or a DVD, or there's still a lot of things in a basement somewhere?

Shyamalan: Not all of them end up. I'm careful not to make the analysis on the Blu-ray so forensic that you, it's hard to watch the movie. So, there's a little calibration that goes on in terms of, let's say for example, there was a character that was cut out, that may or may not be okay for you to watch the movie after you knew that. I want to keep the purity of the movie as much as possible. I don't mind scenes that give you more depth into the characters, so I tend to put those kinds of scenes in the deleted scenes, not every scene that was deleted.

Weintraub: I believe, many years ago, you met with Spielberg about writing a fourth *Indiana Jones* movie. Did you ever come up with your MacGuffin and the idea, or was it more just a basic meeting?

Shyamalan: Oh, my God. I mean, it was fantastic. Obviously *Raiders* is my favorite movie of all time, and so this was a dream, to be asked as a kid to go see a movie in a movie theater and then later to be asked by that person to write one of those in the future. I could faint at that moment. It was amazing. I do have my notebooks, I still have those with all my ideas for that movie. I did have a take. I talked to everybody involved and it was so nascent at that time, that movie. Everyone hadn't gotten into a room yet. They were bouncing ideas off of me. So everyone had different ideas of what to do. When you say that, I have in my head, it's a green notebook, and I had this idea. It was a darker idea.

Weintraub: Every *Indiana Jones* movie has the MacGuffin, so had you thought about what that was yet?

Shyamalan: I did, I did, yeah. I had an idea. I hadn't pitched it to them or anything like that, but I had an idea.

Weintraub: Okay. I won't press you any further. I know that you also expressed interest many years ago in *Harry Potter*. Do you view that as something that got away, or were you like, "These movies are really good, it's cool."

Shyamalan: Oh, definitely. Our kids watched them, and we all watched them and loved them. They have almost a nostalgia about them now, an innocence about them that represented a certain time in filmmaking, I think. I find them beautiful. Obviously I know a lot of them, Rupert's now in my show, so I've always felt close to them when I met them all as kids. I was in my late twenties when I was meeting them and now they're older than I am when I met them. So it's very, it's amazing.

That is more than a job, you have to change your life. You got to move to England and change your whole life. I guess it goes right to the core of, are you making original movies or are you not? There was some really fundamental, when you're making movies of that scale and all of that stuff. Again, talking about all of this, those were early days, but talking about, what type of voice are you and what is the best way to tell those stories where your voice can be your voice? Is it in large-scale movies like that? Does your imagination work that way or does it work in this almost indie way?

Weintraub: Roger Deakins and Steven Soderbergh are famous for very limited coverage onset. They generally have one camera set up, they're getting very limited, almost no coverage. Roger famously shot, I believe, *Blade Runner 2049* and *James Bond* with one camera. I'm curious when you're on set, how much coverage are you trying to do? How much are you just doing the minimal coverage?

Shyamalan: Yeah, there's no coverage per se. We shoot everything that I drew. 99.9999 percent of the time, there isn't anything else that we're doing, it's just the things I drew, and that's what we're shooting, exactly in that way. When Roger and I did *The Village* together, we worked out the shots and that's it. That's what's there. And so, it's play-like. I'm of that mind, entirely, of the old school mentality of, make the movie in your head and go get that movie.

Weintraub: How do you typically like to talk to your actors before they step on set the first day? Are you giving them certain things to watch, certain things to read? What is that dynamic like?

Shyamalan: It varies actor to actor, project to project, but we do rehearse a lot. It's like a theater. On *Old*, it was a very much like a theater group. I would say to them, "Hey, think of the blocking and the movement with your relationship to the camera as dance moves and not as, "Hey, my character would do this," or, "My character would do that." This is the choreography of the movement of the camera, and how I was thinking of it in terms of your positioning in juxtaposition to others and in relationship to the camera. And when you take a step forward, we're moving this way. I see another person, her cheek comes in, all that stuff. Think of it as choreography, and then I'm going to talk you through the emotional meaning of that choreography." Within that seeming structure, there's infinite ways to perform it. So, when it's very complicated choreography, I try to do it early so that they get comfortable with, "Hey, this is how I'm seeing it." And ones that are more fluid like, "Hey, I have a locked-off frame and you can move whatever you want into the bathroom, out of the bathroom, come in." There's a scene where they're—in the movie, where they're fighting and I put a light on a bed and one in the bathroom. I was like, "Go wherever you want. These are the hit points, but you could be—" I said, "You could be entirely in the bathroom and I never see you, if you wanted to do that version of that take." So there's times where I'm like, "Your complete spontaneity is what I'm looking for."

Weintraub: With *Old* it's your first time shooting something out of Philadelphia. Will it be your last time filming something out of Philadelphia?

Shyamalan: I don't think so. The next few movies that I have in my head are kind of, you could shoot them in Philly. One of them takes place in a couple locations outside, but they're very contained. A lot of them could be done the traditional way, but I'm getting more comfortable with writing exterior. And then it's not Philadelphia, normally it's exterior, Philadelphia or interior building, Philadelphia. Probably 'cause my kids have gotten older and I feel the freedom to do that.

Weintraub: One of the things that's interesting about this is that you have different actors playing the same characters. Some of them, I should say. Was there ever, in your mind, like, "Do I want to make it that every fifteen minutes there's going to be a different actor?" Talk about the progression, how you want it to depict that on screen and how much is it, when you have like a movie star or a star that you need to have in the movie, you have to play a little bit more like, "I need this character on screen for an hour, because they're a star and they're helping me sell the movie," versus . . . Does that make any sense?

Shyamalan: Yeah, yeah. I didn't quite think of it, but yes, yes. I didn't quite think of it like that, but there was a math equation here of making sure I wasn't looking at prosthetics the whole movie, that was critical to me. I didn't want that. I didn't want that feeling. I wanted it to be various ways of representing this movement of look and age. I remember, and even now the idea of insinuating people on the edge of frame or being behind them, I thought that was a wonderful way to be provocative with the audience to say, "Well, now the kids are older, but I'm not showing them to you, and what, I wonder what they look like," and you're just getting, "Wow, their hair looks the same, but they don't quite look the same."

That movement of, can I find actors that really look like each other that are fifteen years apart? That they move and they actually can feel like each other. How can we use CGI or prosthetics in very gentle, delicate way that create like, "Wow, I'm seeing them, and that's from that scene to that scene, they're slightly older." Are you catching it, or you might not catch it, that kind of thing. So we analyzed that and every actor got how old they were in every scene. They got a chart of age for every scene that they were.

Weintraub: I don't want to be specific because obviously I don't want to spoil anything, but this is one of those movies that could have ended in a few different places. I think the ending's great, but I'm curious how you ended up where you did because you—and again, it's hard without being specific, but there's a few places where I'm like . . . Was it always this ending, or did you ever have another version of it? Or a different thought of where this could end?

Shyamalan: It was always this ending. For me, the graphic novel, which had no ending essentially and didn't explain anything, had a few frames in it where I thought they were insinuating something. So I kept writing that version of the story of my head. I go, "Ooh, that must mean that. That image of that person over there, that must mean that there's something else going on."

For me, it was very much from the graphic novel, almost like a painting that was unfinished, that they were insinuating what the rest of the painting was. So that ending that you have was from that, it was from that. It was always that version. There were different rhythms of how did to convey that ending, there were various versions of conveying that ending, but it was always that ending.

Jury President M. Night Shyamalan: "The Berlinale Is a Mini Film School"

Andreas Busche / 2022

From *Tagesspiegel* (February 10, 2022). Reprinted by permission of Andreas Busche.

Andreas Busche: Mr. Shyamalan, you're known in Hollywood as a master of surprising last-minute twists. How do you approach your role as jury president? Can we expect a Golden Bear winner that no one had in mind?

M. Night Shyamalan: I have to disappoint you, my taste in films is unfortunately totally predictable, downright boring. But I can't wait to see these eighteen films and discuss them with an incredible group of film enthusiasts. For me, it's like a mini film school.

Busche: The Berlinale is your very first jury job ever, right?

Shyamalan: I've been asked by festivals every now and then, but it never happened due to scheduling. This year, the Berlinale is right between two films in my calendar, so the timing is perfect.

Busche: Are you aware that you are chairing the Berlinale jury exactly twenty years after your Indian colleague Mira Nair?

Shyamalan: Is that true? Wow! I didn't know that. I think our jury is incredible, a wonderful collection of storytellers from all over the world. I can hardly imagine a group of people more diverse than Ryūsuke Hamaguchi, Tsitsi Dangarembga, and Connie Nielsen.

Busche: Mira Nair is one of the very few jury presidents in Berlinale history to come from neither Europe nor the United States. In recent years, Western film festivals have become increasingly diverse. What criteria will you bring into the discussions as jury president?

Shyamalan: I don't like to set criteria in advance. For me personally, what is important in principle is whether filmmakers achieve what they set out to do in the end. It doesn't matter whether it's a nihilistic mountain drama or a romantic comedy. So the more difficult question a jury has to ask is: How do we compare two films of equal quality, but with different ambitions in terms of their goals? I always want to judge directors by their aspirations. Each film presents itself with its own vocabulary, but its quality depends on whether this language has an inner logic that the audience can follow.

Busche: Your films have never been shown at major A-list festivals, and now you're about to make your debut as jury president. Do you also see this as recognition as an auteur filmmaker in Hollywood?

Shyamalan: I've always seen myself as an independent director working within the structures of Hollywood. I'm 3,000 miles away from the film industry here in Philadelphia, and I've been financing my films myself lately. My goal has always been to create something of my own, something original that will be seen by the widest possible audience. At the same time, I feel a great affinity with independent cinema and world cinema, with forms of storytelling that dare to do something new. Film festivals play an important role in promoting these exceptional voices and finding an audience for them.

Busche: Do you see yourself more as a genre director or a dramatic filmmaker who plays with genres?

Shyamalan: I make dramatic films, the genre is just the garb. I think scenes mostly from suspense though, my mind is always working, even now. What is my subject doing at this moment, what is he thinking about, what could be the next question? I love cinema. Nothing means more to me than framing and composing a picture, choosing costumes, planning camera movements, casting actresses from all over the world. And I can only hope that my films radiate a certain ethos that is in a tradition with the cinema I adore.

Busche: As an Indian American director in Hollywood, how do you assess international cinema?

Shyamalan: In the US, we don't have a very good infrastructure for international films; you have to live either in New York or Los Angeles. Outside of these metropolises, it's very difficult to see films from other countries. In Philadelphia we have two arthouse cinemas with small screens, you always have to stay tuned so you don't miss anything. Usually, only films that have exploded internationally arrive here. That's why when I travel, I always try to inform myself about what movies I should definitely see. I also often watch older films to understand how cinema and film language evolved that we take for granted today.

Busche: You were born in India and grew up on the US East Coast. Was your heritage an issue in the US film industry twenty-five years ago?

Shyamalan: Actually, not much has changed; I'm mostly the "other." I look different, my voice sounds different, the trajectory of my career is very particular. It's all part of a package that I stand for as a filmmaker with my work. But in the past few years, more and more films are coming out through which there is a greater understanding that my films no longer need to be judged by categories like "American," "non-American," or "Indian." That's an exciting experience. It's also because of me that my films are difficult to break down into fixed categories. My style, for example, is very European—slow, quiet, and very formal. My camera, on the other hand, is more influenced by classical Japanese cinema. I am an Indian director who grew up in the US—and therefore would have liked to belong to that "club." But my most important lesson is that you can only find your own voice if you stay true to yourself.

Busche: Who was your role model when you started out in Hollywood in the mid-nineties?

Shyamalan: Spike Lee, for sure. I read his book *Gotta Have It: Inside Guerilla Filmmaking* when I was a young kid, and that's what first gave me the idea to seriously pursue this film career. Spike was making independent films when there was no predetermined path for someone like him. He had to find his own way into the industry, from New York at that. That East Coast mindset, which I count the Coen brothers as, appealed to me at the time. I kept telling Spike that if it wasn't for him, I probably would have been a doctor.

Busche: Your parents came to America as doctors. US comedians like Aziz Ansari and Hasan Minhaj like to make jokes about Indian "tiger fathers" and immigrants projecting their own expectations onto their children. What did your parents think when you told them you wanted to be a director?

Shyamalan: The classic Indian reaction: they were disappointed. The idea sounded so absurd to their ears; I could have told them I wanted to be a Christian goth rock singer. They would not have reacted differently. The typical immigrant mentality is: You have to work your way in the system. As opposed to: I want to change the system. My parents thought I was crazy.

Busche: Your parents finally financed your first film *Praying with Anger* from 1992.

Shyamalan: It was a small film, we shot in India with their friends. And it immediately made it to the Toronto festival.

Busche: How do you see your position as an auteur filmmaker in the current Hollywood franchise mania?

Shyamalan: I see things in a more differentiated way now. Actually, not that much has changed. Films with a signature can still find their audience. The difference is that today there is less leniency for filmmakers who have yet to develop their own voice. They lack the safety net. Before the streaming boom, these films were at least given a chance; that doesn't happen anymore. But films that work will always find their audience.

Busche: *The Sixth Sense* was your breakthrough and a blockbuster twenty-three years ago. Today, it would probably just be a respectable success that would get you into the next phase of your career: directing a Marvel movie.

Shyamalan: It was no different back then. After *The Sixth Sense*, I was offered a *Harry Potter* film. I had the choice of doing these commercial films or continuing on my path. I remain optimistic about that. The market is gigantic. Even if my films don't come close to Marvel's success, I still see enough niches for the *Parasite* [2019, from Bong Joon-ho] films of this world.

Busche: This Berlinale is taking place under pandemic conditions. You also shot your latest film *Old* under pandemic conditions on a remote beach. What was that experience like?

Shyamalan: We were very fortunate that the subject of the film (note: a group of people get lost on a deserted beach) allowed us to have a very straightforward production during this difficult time. The shoot took place on schedule over seven weeks with a small crew in the Dominican Republic. We were together all day, living together, being tested regularly. Since the entire country was in shutdown, we only moved between the hotel and the beach. This was right at the beginning of the pandemic, so everyone took the requirements very seriously. That bonded our group together. It was really a formative experience.

"Terrorized by This Light in Us"

Aurélien Lemant / 2022

From *La Septième Obsession* (Hors-Série N° 9, April 2022). Reprinted by permission of Thomas Aïdan and *La Septième Obsession*.

3:00 p.m., Eastern Time. The screen is still black. The connection struggles to be established. The heart is pounding, as if before an overdue movie. A bit like a child who thinks he hears a noise in the darkness, we ask if there is someone. We watch, squinting at the computer that lights up. Then one recognizes the voice, having listened to it dozens of times. A combination of passionate fervor, joy and speed.

The image finally comes. The man shows himself, white shirt and smile, as if for a very long cameo in a sequence shot, facing the camera. And it's nothing to say: even with a banal webcam, even sitting at the office of the HQ where he supervises the preproduction of his next film, M. Night Shyamalan makes an interview, as much as a break, a moment of cinema. This is what happens to those of us who are struck with incandescent cinephilia. The elocution machine-guns its words, in the service of a myriad of concepts, memories and hypotheses. And if the verbal cadence calms down, it is only to better hammer out certain ends of sentences, less like mantras than lines cut for a scene yet to be written. During the interview, on the alert and always listening, Shyamalan will occasionally take notes with a pen, on a sheet of paper, inspired by the conversation and its urgency. Indeed, we will have thirty minutes in all to hear as much as to watch the author of *Sixth Sense* (1999), as hyperactive and meticulous as if he were trying to invent a new project to add to a pile of files that we already imagine too high. The timing, more tenuous than expected—and especially than hoped for—will be officially reduced live by a collaborator at the beginning of the meeting, and measured remotely by a jovial assistant who we will gladly believe to be energetic and in phase with the filmmaker's locomotor flow. Time is short. We will not have the possibility to sort out the questions internally, we will have to follow the stopwatch and react to the second. However, we know that the man who smiles at us is autonomous and talkative, and that he resembles his films, but in a hollow way.

To the dialogic economy and the languor of his dollies for an *Unbreakable* (2000) or an *Old* (2021), will answer an inexhaustible lover of people, overexcited, although master of his eloquence as of his effects. His films are also like him, they and he only speak of quest and abandonment to something higher than oneself. Half an hour to discuss what filmmaking means to him, between focus and suffering, to evoke his politics of actors, his overpowering link to childhood, his conception of innocence and salvation, the notion of genre film, and, more unexpectedly, his spiritual and social investment at the heart of the MNS Foundation that he created in 2001 with his wife, Dr. Bhavna Shyamalan, in order to fight against the growth of poverty and inequality everywhere in this broken world. A world he says we can be the saviors, rather than a cancer. Half an hour inside the head and gestures of the man we call Night.

M. Night Shyamalan: How are you doing?
Aurélien Lemant: I'm doing great! How are you?
Shyamalan: I've never been so busy in my life. I don't know how I've managed, I'm on three projects at the same time! [*Laughs*]
Lemant: Three? I won't ask you to divulge them to us, don't worry! Speaking of projects, you have said that the most successful films are those where every shot is conceived well in advance. On the set, do you ever improvise, change your mind or image completely, or let yourself be guided by a new inspiration?
Shyamalan: There are many ways to create cinema. One is to assemble your ideas as they come, as inspiration strikes: "Oh, let's pull that curtain," "Oh, that way you tapped your fingers on the table, let me shoot that," etc. You gather the ingredients to make your own cooking, but what comes out will be decided later, when you're editing: "Here's that shot where she's tapping on the table, let's focus on that. Let's cut to here, right after a shot of the actress' face, and bang, we build the whole scene around her hand on the table." Stunning films have come out of this way of doing things, rooted in the moment, spontaneity, à la Cassavetes; you leave room for the film to emerge in the middle of it all. The other way, which is perhaps rarer, although of course many people have used it, is to structure the entire narrative in your head, before rendering it on celluloid. You wonder how a character will appear for the first time on the screen, what the exact rhythm of the camera movement will be that will reveal it to us, what this specific movement tells us about the character's profile, how to find out who he is talking to, and why he is making a certain decision. You spend all your time imagining the right light in the background, imagining every single item on his shelf, how the character is dressed, wondering if the color of his clothes will stand out on the desk he is sitting at.

All of your thoughts converge on doing that thing you have in mind, which boils down to: "What appears on the screen?" Right now, everyone who is in this building with me working on this new film is working in that direction. They might say to me, "You know, that gardener that comes in in sequence 35, maybe we can see him a little bit earlier in the picture, through a window. [*He turns to the window behind him, as if he is going to appear outside at the bottom of the garden behind him.*] He is there, and his clothes would be of a color that is inevitably noticeable, so that the viewer wonders if this is a disturbing character or not, but we will only know later in the story." And so on, all converging on the same goal. [*He holds up a thick binder full of drawings in front of his webcam (a storyboard).*] That's just under five months, eighteen weeks spent drawing the future film. It's grueling! Back-breaking! And we do it again! And we do it again! "That doesn't work! What is this thing? Oh my!" We can't use the zoom for this scene, we've developed a language for the film, so we have to respect it. I design the whole set according to the shots to be shot, not the other way around; so it's crucial to imagine beforehand how we're going to show this thing or that thing. This way of proceeding is very painful, but it is mine. Because that's how my mind works. Painful, because you have to think everything out in advance. There is still inspiration, but it is in the service of an already well-defined destination. On set, we'll eventually say, "What if we light in an ultra-geometric or expressionistic way when so-and-so opens the kitchen door," because that improvised idea serves the scene. And when the time comes to shoot it, I have to do everything so that the actors' interpretation, the camera movements, the light, everything, in short, is directed towards this destination. I like to explain to my actors why I film a certain scene in a certain way. Like his character, the actor believes he is in control, but in reality, he is not in control of anything; his character's life is about to spiral out of control, yet he hangs on as best he can to what he has left. In 99.99 percent of the cases, the actor loves it, he totally accepts it because it's thought from A to Z to stimulate his performance. I then tell him that the camera will only start to move when he starts to doubt and his varnish cracks, that's how we will succeed in our shot. The camera will start to move when the actor is destabilized, not before. The actors are very enthusiastic when they hear these kinds of remarks.

Lemant: Wow! But then, you yourself, do you feel on the set shooting like that?

Shyamalan: You know what? It's such a meticulous job that it's nerve-wracking. I feel two states during a shoot. When I'm in pain. And when I'm not in pain [*laughs*]. When I'm out of pain, we check the gate and move on to the next shot [*laughs*].

Lemant: What is the first thing you ask an actor in front of the camera, or even before?

Shyamalan: I'm starting a film right now so it's a process I'm mentally preparing for. First of all, I need the right cast. I'm casting people who have auditioned that I've worked with on a previous film, so I know their energy pretty intimately. I connect with them, where they are now in their lives, because an actor was not the same as he is today three years ago. His energy is not in the same place. What did he work on? What have been his new experiments? I try to find people with exceptional physical condition. They'll have to be hyper-prepared. No "I don't know my lines," none of that. I try to set up rehearsals early in the production to generate a sense of small community, staying as far away from contract negotiations as possible. When an actor needs direction, I say, "Look, I'm going to challenge you, it's going to be hard, I'm very focused, I'm shooting really tightly, in thirty-three, thirty-five, thirty-eight days. I'm going to put everything aside for the film during those days. Allow yourself the risk of failure with me, you won't collapse, give yourself every opportunity to become more flexible, don't be closed. My goal is to find out where your comfort zone is and to go just a little bit beyond it." We are always either expanding or contracting, we never stay the same. I describe to the actors the choreography of my sequence. I've spent my whole life doing that, since childhood, saying to them, "Think of it as dance, what do you mean when you extend your hand," like a choreographer would ask them. "Stay open to this process, I'm going to push you to assert your emotion within this choreographed movement." It's beautiful and it's going to become a different artistic expression through a discipline that is rooted in a particularly consistent vocabulary. I've had all these discussions with the actors. It speaks to them. And right now I'm telling them, "It's great if it's something you're not comfortable with for once [*laughs*]. The seventeen projects that you're going to be involved in, everyone around you is going to make sure that it's going to go the way you're used to. So maybe you might like the one I'm proposing. Discover this way of telling stories." And when you see my previous films, you realize that it's a very specific job. I assume that if you look at the features of my peers, Wes Anderson, Quentin [Tarantino], or whoever, there's a strong emphasis on something special every time, and that's what the audience expects, that way of thinking about cinema. The actors are usually so excited about it! That's the case with the group I've assembled to launch this new project. They're excited about what is almost a kind of play/cinema at the heart of our storytelling.

Lemant: It must come from that, your actors are all so intense, even when filmed from behind. Something strong comes out of their necks, their skulls, even when the camera doesn't move for a moment. I don't remember seeing this in such a pronounced way in others. It's like a signature.

Shyamalan: When you witness great acting, it emanates from every cell in the actor's body. If an actor has to do a scene and he's on his seventh take, there's no way he's going to think exactly the same or his body is going to reproduce the action in exactly the same way. After a while, he imitates what he did in the third take because he felt good in that moment, and he reproduces that action in the following takes. Also, I know that he's not really where he needs to be, emotionally speaking. So I'm very restrictive about everything on their canvas, but in these cases I force the actors to be as messy and organic as possible within the confines of the canvas. On the eighth take, I'll say to the actor, "Okay, this time you're not allowed to do anything that you've already proposed in the other takes, you can't have the thoughts that you've already had, you're not allowed to do that anymore. All right, let's go again, motor!" And then the actors start shouting, "What?!" [*Laughs*] Then they get to this singular game, and I ask them, "Ah, did you see how you managed to get angry during that love scene? Go on, keep it up! It came to you naturally. Power!" The scene then becomes a bit of a mess, and if the frame is pretty tight, the actors won't respect their marks on the floor, they'll go out of frame like that. [*He moves to the side so that his face is almost out of the field of his webcam.*] The cinematographer is going to try to correct it [*he moves his webcam to crop himself*] and I'm going to start yelling, "What are you doing? Don't fucking crop! [*Laughs*] Her character is angry, so she's out of frame! Do you understand?" The question is always how to use that tension between the preconceived and the spontaneous, to create this beautiful juxtaposition.

Lemant: And with the children on your shoots, does it work too?

Shyamalan: Again, if you cast the right person, if you pay attention to the values that govern the group that you've gathered like a family around the child, if you stay mindful of how you approach that child, how the actors approach each other, if you throw the right energy from your soul at a child, on set they are always going to have that messy side that I'm looking for, so I never have to worry about that. I'm not going to be as restrictive as I am with adults, I'm not going to demand that they stand up, that they put their arm down, I'm going to tell them to stand behind that couch and at some point, I'm just going to need them to go and get the candy that's on the chair. When I make that little gesture behind the camera [*he waves his hand*], they will be allowed to go, they may even anticipate to change the rhythm of the scene, and so on. We play together, as human beings. I love working with kids, at least the ones I connect with through their roles when they are really close to who they really are, the ones with whom you can capture unpredictable moments laughing at the formalist camera frame. It's beautiful.

Lemant: It's funny, because a lot of your adult heroes have something childlike about them—it's not about maturity, but about preserving a certain innocence.

Shyamalan: We know that children are closer to the Universe, maybe to God, some people say. They are compared to angels because they let go naturally. We have forgotten how they do it. Those of us who are lucky enough to find inner balance, peace, meditation, Grace, a God, whatever, learn to let go again. And so these actors who manage to embody characters who let go in all circumstances, who accept, who open up, it's such a beautiful example to watch, it's a chance. What attracts me to so-called genre films is not the genre as such, it's the potentials that the characters have to face. The supernatural, as a key element of the genre film, is a means of acceptance and letting go for them. They see the world again through the eyes of a child.

Lemant: We feel in your films that you need answers.

Shyamalan: I like puzzles. There's something about solving puzzles that's like rebalancing. [*He turns his webcam to 180º, unfolding the wall in front of his desk, against which are displayed colorful photographs.*] Here is a wall on which I have put images for this new film. They represent various things, I don't even know how to articulate them. Why is this child lying with her father beside her? It reminds me of the notion of negative space; there is a kind of movement, a beautiful balance that, for me, suggests a puzzle. I'm trying to understand and solve this puzzle whose question is, "What is the puzzle?" How do I balance the new film I'm going to make? But it's so nice to get to that point where you see beauty in everything. That's life, you know?

Lemant: Your cinema is constantly a cinema of salvation. It's not just about solving a mystery, but a spiritual quality.

Shyamalan: That's me. I live things in a very positive way. But I'm also a dark person. I don't shy away from suffering. I don't deny this dark side, I face it. However, there is nothing in this world in which I do not find a part of light. For example, our foundation works with many people in Syria. When I've talked to people there, who have seen and experienced the worst of it, mass murder on a scale we can't fathom, I've told them how incredible they are. I don't just tell them, I believe it! I saw tears welling up in their eyes, and I said, "You are a miracle! You are here, and you still manage to love, to smile? Evil had no chance to succeed! No chance! Look at you! Evil has made you see everything and you still have love in your eyes." Our part of humanity will not only survive, it will grow.

Lemant: Kevin Wendell Crumb, with his multiple personalities, is a creature that combines everything you just brought up in terms of darkness and light.

Shyamalan: All these personalities are there to protect Kevin. They don't want to recognize that they are all him. They think, "Oh, poor Kevin! He's been through a lot." I haven't been through his problems, I'm very devout and very clean, and nothing bad has ever happened to me. Teach Kevin to clean up his act and he will be safer. Kevin's personalities need to believe that they can preserve him. It's interesting because when I studied this dissociative identity disorder, I found it poignant. It's understandable that I see this disorder as a superpower, that of an individual who, in order to survive, creates his own community within himself. He sees his other personalities as heroes protecting his core identity. We are all extremely powerful beings. Adulthood and society have taken that knowledge away from us. I reminded the people in Syria who are fighting against [Bashar] al-Assad. They don't realize that what they are accomplishing is just incredible for the world. We are all capable of that. We have forgotten it, or we are terrorized by this light in us.

Further Reading

Bamberger, Michael. *The Man Who Heard Voices: Or, How M. Night Shyamalan Risked His Career on a Fairy Tale*. New York: Gotham Books, 2006.

Cerezo, Raúl, and José Colmenarejo. *M. Night Shyamalan: El cineaste de cristal*. Córdoba: Berenice, 2019.

Derole, Hugues, ed. *Contes de l'au-delà: Le cinéma de M. Night Shyamalan*. Paris: Vendémiaire, 2015.

Deschamps, Youri, ed. *M. Night Shyamalan: Derrière les images*. Eclipses (Caen), no. 61, 2017.

Gmelch, Adrian. *Die Neuerfindung des M. Night Shyamalan*. Marburg: Büchner Verlag, 2021.

Weinstock, Jeffrey Andrew, ed. *Critical Approaches to the Films of M. Night Shyamalan: Spoiler Warnings*. New York: Palgrave Macmillan, 2010.

Zywietz, Bernd. *Tote Menschen sehen: M. Night Shyamalan und seine Filme*. Band 1. Mainz: Edition Screenshot, 2008.

Index

ABC, 37
Affleck, Ben, 10
Air Force One, 6
Al-Assad, Bashar, 140
Alien, 44, 47, 122
Allen, Woody, 10, 55
Altman, Robert, 47, 117–18
Alvin and the Chipmunks: The Squeakquel, 101
Ambat, Madhu, 4
Anderson, Wes, 137
Ansari, Aziz, 132
Aronofsky, Darren, 92
Attack of the Clones, 21
Austin Powers in Goldmember, 21
Awakenings, 10

Balaban, Bob, 56–57
Bamberger, Michael, 51, 87
Barnsley, Michael, 59
Barton, Mischa, 98
Basic Instinct, 6
Batman, 84
Battleship Earth, 34
Bay, Michael, 28
Benedek, Peter, 6, 10
Bergman, Ingmar, 20
Birds, The, 47, 64
Blade Runner 2049, 127
Blair Witch Project, The, 37
Blind Side, The, 90

Blink, 51
Blum, Jason, 107, 108, 110–11
Bordwell, David, xi
Braveheart, 102
Breslin, Abigail, 20
Brody, Adrien, 38, 41
Brontë, Emily, 36
Buckley, Betty, 69
Buddhism, 52, 58, 72, 81
Burdeau, Emmanuel, xi
Burton, Tim, 47

Cameron, James, 61, 81
Capra, Frank, 10
Carrie, 32
Cassavetes, John, 135
Celebrity, 10
Chazelle, Damien, 108
Christie, Agatha, 57
Chronicles of Narnia, The, 71
Clerks, 10
Clinton, Bill, 51, 100
Close Encounters, 51
Coen brothers, 6, 82, 89, 132
Columbia Pictures, 3, 6
Conrad, Joseph, 43
Cook, Richard, 21, 37
Coppola, Francis Ford, 31, 91
Crouching Tiger, Hidden Dragon, 85
Crystal Trap, 47
Culkin, Rory, 20

Dalai Lama, 81
Damon, Matt, 10
Dangarembga, Tsitsi, 130
Dante DiMartino, Michael (Mike), 74–78, 79, 80
D'Antonio, Michael, 12
Davis, Andrew, 44
Deakins, Roger, 39, 48, 127
Deconstructing Harry, 10
DeMonaco, James, 108
De Palma, Brian, 32
Departed, The, 64
Deschanel, Zooey, 67
Devil's Candy, The, 51
Die Hard, 29
Dillon, Matt, 94
Disney, Walt, 37
Disney Pictures, 5, 20, 21, 24, 27, 37, 41, 50, 51, 87, 91, 116
Dogtooth, 108
Dylan, Bob, 50

Edward Scissorhands, 47
Einstein, Albert, 67–68
Einstein: His Life and Universe, 67
El Mariachi, 3
Eszterhas, Joe, 6
E.T., x, 7, 25, 60, 63, 99
Exorcist, The, x, 6, 25, 32, 47

Fellini, Federico, 20
Fighter, The, 90
Fox, David M., 4
Franklin, Benjamin, 31
Freud, Sigmund, 33
Friday the 13th, 40
Friends, 122
Fujimoto, Tak, 64

Gandhi, 7
Ghost, 100

Giamatti, Paul, 49, 54, 56, 57, 107
Gibson, Mel, 19–20, 21, 22, 61, 75, 88, 93, 102
Gioulakis, Mike, 117, 120
Gladwell, Malcolm, 51
Glick, Marc H., 20
Godfather, The, 91
Good Will Hunting, 10
Grey, Brad, 73
Grinch, The, 25
Grint, Rupert, 126
Guinness Book of World Records, 40

Hamaguchi, Ryūsuke, 130
Hanson, Curtis, 6
Harry Potter, 52, 71, 126, 133
Heart of Darkness, 43
Help, The, 90
Hinduism, 6, 22, 30, 40, 43, 52, 58, 67, 72, 81
Hitchcock, Alfred, x, xi, 17, 20, 28, 43, 55, 64, 93, 121, 122, 123
Hollinger, Meg, 19
Horn, Alan, 91
Howard, Bryce Dallas, 37, 49
Howard, James Newton, 63, 84
Howard, Ron, 40
Howard, Terrence, 94
Hughes, John, 10
Hurt, William, 38, 39, 41, 47

Independence Day, 62
Indiana Jones, 126. See also *Raiders of the Lost Arc*; *Temple of Doom*
In the Blink of an Eye, 119
Invasion of the Body Snatchers, 47
Iron Man, 84, 86
Irons, Jeremy, 29
Isaacson, Walter, 67

Jackson, Samuel L., 17, 29, 32, 75, 115
Jacobson, Nina, 38, 51

James Bond, 21, 40, 99, 127
Jaws, x, 25, 51, 90, 121
John Adams, 95
Jordan, Michael, 51, 69, 77, 92
Jurassic Park, 62, 78

Kasdan, Jake, 10
King, Stephen, 37, 66
King Kong, 47
Kingsley, Ben, 84
Konietzko, Bryan, 74–78, 80
Kurosawa, Akira, 20

Lanthimos, Yorgos, 108
Lasseter, John, 44, 51
Leary, Denis, 9
Lee, Ang, 31
Lee, Spike, 4, 43, 50, 64, 88–89, 132
Leguizamo, John, 67
Levinson, Barry, 108
Lewis, Juliette, 94
Life of Pi, 52, 78
Lincoln, Abraham, 50
Lion King, The, 6
"Little Red Riding Hood," 47
Loggia, Robert, 9, 10
Lord of the Rings, The, 77, 78, 85
Lucas, George, 20, 31, 46, 78
Lucky Numbers, 33
Luhrmann, Baz, 9

Mandela, Nelson, 85–86
Man Who Heard Voices, The, 51, 87
Martin, Paul, 50
Mason, Bobbie Ann, 29
Mason, Brick, 28, 47
Masters, Kim, 57
McAvoy, James, 108, 111, 113, 115
McCabe & Mrs. Miller, 47
McTiernan, John, 3
Mendel, Barry, 24

Meyler, Katie, 97
Minhaj, Hasan, 132
Minkoff, Rob, 6
Miyazaki, Hayao, 77
M. Night Shyamalan Foundation (MNSF), x, 88, 95–97, 139
Moffat, Steven, 101
Moonstruck, 3
Moore, Demi, 100
Murch, Walter Scott, 119

Nair, Mira, 130
New York University (NYU), 3, 4, 7, 8, 12, 22, 40, 50, 65, 87, 95, 96
Nickelodeon, 61, 73, 74, 75
Nielsen, Connie, 130
Nightmare on Elm Street, A, 99
Night of the Living Dead, 47

O'Donnell, Rosie, 6, 9, 23–24
Office, The, 122
One Flew over the Cuckoo's Nest, 47, 117
Ordinary People, 6
Osment, Haley Joel, 19, 24, 32, 44

Pan's Labyrinth, 70
Parasite, 133
Patel, Dev, 75
Paulson, Sarah, 117
Peeping Tom, 112
Peltz, Nicola, 84
Perfect Storm, The, 73
Petersen, Wolfgang, 6
Phoenix, Joaquin, 20, 41, 45, 61, 107
Picture, 51
Pirates of the Caribbean, 90
Pokémon, 22
Ponyo, 77
Powell, Michael, 112
Primetime Live, 37

Psycho, 93
Puzo, Mario, 91

Raiders of the Lost Ark, 7, 22, 24, 47, 63, 64, 79, 88, 121, 126
Rebecca, 122
Reiner, Rob, 3
Ringer, Noah, 80, 81, 83
Rodriguez, Robert, 9
Romero, George A., 44
Ross, Lillian, 51
Rudin, Scott, 36, 40

Salamon, Julie, 51
Sayles, John, 52
Schindler's List, 10
Scorsese, Martin, 5, 16, 64
Searching for Bobby Fischer, 10, 83
Seinfeld, 69, 92, 122
Semanick, Michael, 21, 22
Serra, Eduardo, 12, 14–15, 16
Sherlock, 101
Shyamalan, Bhavna, x, 5, 8, 22–23, 24, 40, 95–97, 135
Shyamalan, Jayalakshmi, 6, 20, 98
Shyamalan, M. Night: on American Indian culture, 40, 67; on artistic integrity, xii, 22, 79, 104; on basketball, 22, 30, 32, 40; on being an auteur, 77, 105, 131, 132; on CGI, 72, 73–74, 120, 128; on changing his middle name, 40, 67; on children in his films, 13, 32–33, 99–100, 125, 138–39; on confidence, 17, 62, 110; on the COVID-19 pandemic, 123, 133; on creativity, 18, 92, 101, 124; on critics, 56, 60, 92, 101–2, 103–4, 105–6; on emotion in films, xi, 3, 5, 14, 15–16, 29, 41, 45, 55, 70, 72, 85, 113–14, 125, 127; on faith, x, xi, 36, 39, 43, 46–47, 49, 51, 52, 59, 68, 81; on family, xi, 13, 23, 31, 36, 46, 52, 61, 63, 67, 103, 104, 107, 112; on favorite filmmakers, 3, 91, 92; on favorite movies, 32, 79, 91, 107, 117, 121, 122, 126; on framing/the right frame, 15, 17, 36, 44–45, 127, 128, 138; on genre, 56, 91, 104, 131, 139; on his European style, 14, 132; on Hollywood film industry, x, 3, 6, 9–10, 15, 23, 52, 100–101, 131–32; on India, 4, 23, 30, 50, 131–32; on karate, 11, 51; on making a B movie, 69; on music, 48, 65, 84–85; on nature, 40, 67, 72; on Philadelphia, x, 10, 30–31, 58–59, 95, 111, 127–28, 131; on the power of and love for cinema, 89, 118, 131; on religion, 30, 40, 46, 58, 60, 67, 68, 81, 102, 119; on Rubik's Cube, 40, 99, 101; on self-financing his films, 120, 125, 131; on sex, xi, 3, 20, 109; on shooting on digital, 65, 119–20; on sound, 21, 22, 48, 70; on spirituality, 30, 40, 47, 67, 69, 72, 77, 119, 139; on storyboarding, 13, 15, 28, 39, 43–44, 47, 81, 136; on storytelling, xi, 57, 72, 106, 131, 137; on superheroes, 105, 106, 116–17; on the supernatural, 13, 101, 139; on television and TV series, 46, 78, 89, 92, 94, 106, 107, 122; on twist endings, 51, 59, 66, 99, 101; on the use of colors, 15, 45, 47, 119, 136; on the use of long takes, 118–19

Works By: *After Earth*, 103, 116, 120; *Black Sheep* (unproduced), 4; *Devil*, 88, 90; *Glass*, 115–20; *The Happening*, 62–65, 67–70, 92, 105; *I Got Schooled*, 94; *Labor of Love* (unproduced), 6, 8, 23, 121, 125; *Lady in the Water*, 50–52, 54–56, 59, 60, 91, 101–2, 105–6,

107; *The Last Airbender*, 64, 71–86, 90, 103, 116; *Old*, 123–24, 127–29, 133; *Praying with Anger*, 3–4, 8, 9, 23, 41, 103, 132; *Signs*, 20–22, 25, 29, 45, 46, 47, 55–56, 58–59, 60, 63, 72, 82, 93, 104, 105, 107, 123; *The Sixth Sense*, 9, 13, 14, 24, 27, 29, 32, 33, 47, 55, 56, 59, 69, 83, 90, 97, 98, 103, 104, 125; *Split*, 108–13, 115, 116, 118, 120, 125, 139; *Stuart Little*, 6, 9, 99, 103, 105; *Unbreakable*, 13–17, 25, 28, 31, 41, 51, 55–56, 62, 82, 85, 92, 104, 105, 106, 107, 115–16, 119, 123; *The Village*, 35, 37, 39, 44, 45–47, 55, 69, 93, 101, 104, 127; *The Visit*, 103–6, 110, 120; *Wayward Pines*, 107; *Wide Awake*, 6, 7, 8, 9, 10, 14, 23–24, 28, 32, 41, 55, 105
Shyamalan, Nelliate C., 6, 22, 98
Shyamalan, Saleka, 5, 9
Shyamalan, Veena, 6, 98
Silence of the Lambs, The, 15, 24, 121
Smith, Kevin, 10
Smith, Will, 51, 67, 88, 89, 100, 108
Soderbergh, Steven, 127
Sopranos, The, 122
Spider-Man 2, 37
Spielberg, Steven, x, 5, 7, 12, 20, 28, 30, 43, 49, 51, 52, 63, 88, 121, 126
Spike Lee's Gotta Have It: Inside Guerilla Filmmaking, 4, 50, 64, 89, 132
Star Wars, 7, 21, 73, 80
Stone, Oliver, 3
Stowe, Harriet Beecher, 50
Strickland, Bob, 5
Swayze, Patrick, 100

Tarantino, Quentin, 9, 10, 137
Taylor-Joy, Anya, 108, 109, 113
Temple of Doom, 74
Thompson, Anne, 51, 52
3 Women, 118
Toub, Shaun, 84

Uncle's Tom Cabin, 50
Universal Pictures, ix, 111

Vaswani, Bhavna. *See* Shyamalan, Bhavna

Wahlberg, Mark, 64, 67, 68
Walters-Michalec, Jennifer, 96, 97
Warner Bros., 51, 88, 91
Weaver, Sigourney, 38, 39, 41
Weinstein, Harvey, 9, 10–11, 23–24, 41
West, Kanye, 51
Williams, Robin, 100
Willis, Bruce, 6, 9, 10, 12, 15, 17, 19, 20, 25, 29, 75, 82, 90, 99, 115, 116, 121, 125
Winfrey, Oprah, 51
Wings of the Dove, The, 15
Witch, The, 108
Woods, Tiger, 51
Working Girl, 8
Wuthering Heights, 36
Wyeth, Andrew, 35, 38

XXX, 21

Zaillian, Steven, 10
Zero Effect, 10
Zimmer, Hans, 84

About the Editor

Photo credit: © Adrian Gmelch

Adrian Gmelch works in corporate marketing. Since he could see and hear, he has had one hobby: film. Gmelch has not only made short films himself but also writes film reviews and articles. He has also given free rein to his hobby on Wikipedia, writing hundreds of articles focusing on film and television, including those surrounding M. Night Shyamalan and David Lynch. Some of them have been awarded the title "good article" by the community. With *Die Neuerfindung des M. Night Shyamalan* (2021), he has published the first monograph on Shyamalan in the German-speaking world. In his book *Art-Horror* (2023), he focuses on the films of Ari Aster and Robert Eggers.

www.ingramcontent.com/pod-product-compliance
Lightning Source LLC
Chambersburg PA
CBHW021844220426
43663CB00005B/390